PRAISE FOR WOMEN OF REDEMPTION

The journey of motherhood surfaces deep emotions that can range from both soul-bursting joy to earth-shattering hopelessness. *Women of Redemption* is an inspiring piece that connects today's woman to our biblical counterparts and reminds us that God's path for us has an intimate purpose, even in our most difficult moments. There is no doubt you will find an instant connection to the vulnerable moments shared by Stephanie and Shannon. The words in this book will not only bless and encourage you, but they will deepen your faith in the Lord's plan for your entire life.

— ERIN CRAFT, MOTHER AND OWNER OF 3 WILLOWS BOUTIQUE

Family is God's idea. In a culture that has diluted the meaning of family (more specifically, Godly family), Shannon and Stephanie take us back to the high calling of motherhood. By revisiting the lives of eight biblical matriarchs and interweaving those experiences with their own, they remind us that we can, by God's grace, be godly mothers in an ungodly world. Women who have any connection with children—not only mothers, but teachers, relatives, and friends as well—will find this book both informative and inspirational.

— REV. REBECCA PETERSON, MOTHER AND RETIRED METHODIST MINISTER

This book will touch the lives of so many world-weary women, both mommas and those who mother others. With so many expectations on women in this world, Stephanie and Shannon offer a magical space of grace for us through these biblical mommas. A space where Jesus holds us close, tells us how precious we are, and helps us, in turn, love fiercely to instruct and protect and love big enough to let go when the time comes.

— AMY SMITH, MOTHER, AUTHOR AND
OWNER OF THE EVERGREEN

Shannon and Stephanie offer a refreshing take on the beauty and complexity of motherhood. Through examining women in the Bible, they shed light on the nuances and uniqueness of each journey, connecting these stories to the diverse tapestry of motherhood today. With joy and care, they leave the reader feeling seen and encouraged, able to embrace their own journey of motherhood. A must-read for all women who take on mothering roles!

— KELLY HAMILTON, MOTHER AND
FOUNDER/EXECUTIVE DIRECTOR OF THE
CONNECTED LIFE

Within reading just a few pages, I already felt encouraged not only as a woman of faith but as a believer trying to navigate through some very interesting times. As a creative business owner and mom, the thoughts shared about dreaming big hit my heartstrings. I believe this book will encourage all female believers.

— CARA FOX, MOTHER AND OWNER OF THE
LITTLE GOLDEN FOX

Women of Redemption is a journey through the lives of eight biblical mothers with lessons for modern-day women. Shannon and Stephanie aren't afraid to tackle hard, raw topics that women in this time struggle with, and show us how women of the Bible fought the same battles. The wisdom of these women and the message that Shannon and Stephanie share bring hope to a hard season of life—any mother struggling with the demands of today's world should read and be renewed!

— BRETT WERST, MOTHER AND FICTION
AUTHOR

As I read this book, I was able to relate to each of these heroic biblical women. The writers' sweet empathy for these iconic ladies of history made it feel as though I were an eyewitness to their trials as well as their victories. And I was able to see the similarities between their experiences and my own. From their struggles and doubts to their epic faithfulness, we find out why God chose these women to be an example for us modern-day mommas.

— BELINDA SHEELEY, MOTHER AND
AUTHOR

This book is a soothing balm for my motherly soul. As a mother of four boys, I often question my role and if I am enough for them. Reading about the experiences of the biblical mothers who went before me was a sweet reminder that I am chosen for such time as this... despite my brokenness and shortcomings. This is a MUST read not just for mothers, but for all women who need supernatural HOPE that there is purpose in the pain.

— SUMMER CRAWFORD, MOTHER AND
OWNER OF SUMMER CRAWFORD DESIGN

WOMEN OF REDEMPTION
MOTHERHOOD WISDOM FROM 8 BIBLICAL MATRIARCHS

SHANNON CARROLL

STEPHANIE FEGER

Women of Redemption: Motherhood Wisdom from 8 Biblical Matriarchs

Cover Design by Madelyn Copperwaite, MC Creative LLC
Cover Artwork by Cat Johnston
Editing by Jennifer Crosswhite, Tandem Services Ink
Layout by emPower PR Group

First edition, April 2024
ISBN (eBook): 979-8-9904866-0-7
ISBN (Paperback): 979-8-9904866-1-4
Library of Congress Control Number: 2024907089
Created in the United States of America

Scripture quotations marked (ESV) are from The Holy Bible, English Standard Version®, Copyright © 2001 by Crossway, a publishing ministry of Good News Publishers. Used by permission. All rights reserved.

Scripture quotations marked (KJV) are from the King James Version, public domain.

Scripture quotations marked (MSG) are from The Message. Copyright © 1993, 1994, 1995, 1996, 2000, 2001, 2002. Used by permission of NavPress Publishing Group.

Scripture quotations marked (NASB) are from the New American Standard Bible®, Copyright © 1960, 1962, 1963, 1968, 1971, 1972, 1973, 1975, 1977, 1995 by The Lockman Foundation. Used by permission.

Scripture quotations marked (NIV) are from The Holy Bible, New International Version®, NIV®. Copyright © 1973, 1978, 1984, 2011 by Biblica, Inc.™ Used by permission of Zondervan.

Scriptures taken from the Holy Bible, New International Reader's Version®, NIrV® Copyright © 1995, 1996, 1998, 2014 by Biblica, Inc.™ Used by permission of Zondervan.

Scripture quotations marked (NLT) are from The Holy Bible, New Living Translation, Copyright © 1996, 2004, 2015 by Tyndale House Foundation. Used by permission of Tyndale House Publishers, Carol Stream, Illinois 60188. All rights reserved.

Learn more about Broken & Beautiful Retreats, LLC and how Shannon and Stephanie can support you, your church and your community by visiting www.BrokenandBeautifulRetreats.com. Learn more about other published works by visiting www.Brokenand-BeautifulPress.com Special discounts are available on quantity book purchases. Contact brokenbeautifulretreats@gmail.com for more information.

CONTENTS

Behind every child is a mother who is doing her best. Despite feelings of failure, inadequacy and worry, she is trying to pave a future for her child that is a bit more level than the rocky path she navigated. Behind the smiles are countless nights of worry. Underneath the concealer are dark circles from hardships. Beneath the strong exterior is a fragile woman trying to hold herself and everything else together.

Deep breath, Momma. God sees all of you—your beautiful and your broken pieces—and loves every part! He chose you for the important task of being your child's mother, and He believes in you even when you may not believe in yourself. And, His faith in you matters most.

This book is dedicated to each and every mother who is ready to surrender the belief that she can tackle motherhood alone. Perfection isn't required; walking in lockstep with God is. These biblical mothers before us offer our stories hope. And the mothers who come after us will, too, be inspired by our steps. May this book offer you a starting point to find your breath again and rest in Him.

He's got this, friend. And, He's got you too.

GOD LOVES MOTHERS

Motherhood. There are almost as many layers of motherhood as there are living and breathing mothers in our world. (Last we checked, according to the United States Census Bureau[1], that's a whopping two billion mothers out there! Just saying.) Motherhood isn't confined to a box; it can take many forms and include every woman, whether or not she's given birth to or adopted children. Grandmothers, aunts, sisters, friends, mothers, stepmothers, foster mothers, adoptive mothers—we all are called to support and raise the next generation. This is such a high calling and one we don't take lightly.

The book you hold in your hands is a compilation of our personal stories of motherhood through the powerful lens of eight mothers in the Bible. Each step in our motherhood journey shapes us, and the steps of mothers before us have the power to as well. As we share our vulnerable moments of motherhood with you—through glazed eyes filled with tears, laugh-out-loud moments recalling memories and bruised knees from the many times we've fallen and gotten back up again—our prayer is that you'll see many correlations with your motherhood journey and those of eight biblical mothers who walked before us.

Like you, Sarah, Hagar, Jochebed, Bathsheba, the Shunammite Woman, Elizabeth, Mary and the Canaanite Woman have motherhood stories that matter, and our hope is that their stories come alive for you as they have for us in our studies. Some of these mothers are obscure, not part of the popular biblical motherhood crowd, which made their stories even more intriguing as we dug to find the nuggets of why God decided to include their testimony in His Word and in this book.

GOD LOVES MOTHERS

Motherhood is a special role He's crafted us to fill; no man can completely step into the place a mother holds. Our heart, our nature, our intuition are unique and specially designed to nurture and equip our sons and daughters for their own life's mission. He chose us to care for His children, and those are some pretty big shoes to fill. (Good news. God believes we are highly capable!)

As you navigate through these stories, grab a box of tissues, pull out a notebook, cuddle up with a blanket and sip a warm cup of whatever you love most, and rest in the messages as you hear God speaking to you. We encourage you to use this book as a devotional, taking your time to let the stories and principles sink deep within your heart.

So, we invite you to...

Laugh with us.
Wipe your tears with us.
Ponder God's purpose with us.
Wonder alongside us.
Ask hard questions with us.
Seek biblical answers with us.
Be vulnerable and honest like us.

Raw and real. That's who we are, and that's what you'll find in each chapter; a vulnerable edge to our writing, we hope, helps you peer into these biblical mother's lives with a new and possibly unusual angle. Unless it's noted differently, the concepts captured came through our own inspired study of Scripture as we viewed each mother's story through our motherhood experiences and understanding.

We are grateful for the scores of pastors and Christian teachers who helped inspire us as we watched multiple sermons, read oodles of articles and researched details to bring to life each of these biblical heroes. Truly God's Living Word is so rich, and we can't wait to spend eternity learning more about each of these women! We often talk about wanting to sit and have coffee with Jochebed or Bathsheba or the other mothers in this book; there are so many details not shared about their situations in Scripture, and we want to know their full story. Someday we will—and we can't wait!

This book is bathed in encouragement, grace and truth, because we recognize that the path of motherhood is not for the faint of heart; it will test us beyond our perceived abilities and push us more than we sometimes want to be pushed. We mothers battle discouragement and feelings of not being good enough daily. We see our time with our children as fleeting and wonder what we could have done differently when they were younger. Sometimes we feel alone, unseen, unimportant. We seek to offer you tools for your toolbelt to battle those voices and lies from the enemy. Strong mothers produce strong families, which impacts communities, nations and even eternity!

> Let us not lose heart in doing good, for in due time we will
> reap if we do not grow weary.
> Galatians 6:9 (NASB)

Whether you're reading through this book with a friend or studying it in the quiet of your own home, we pray you'll receive encouragement to keep on keeping on in your motherhood story. No matter the stage of life you're in, there's something in these pages to inspire and challenge you. We believe it! God has chosen *you* to bear, raise and influence the children in your life, and He's especially equipped you to fulfill that calling.

You are making a difference for all of eternity.
You are leaving a legacy for the next generation.
You are worth it and worthy of it.
You are doing your best, and you're changing and shaping lives in the process.

Be blessed, sweet mother!

Shannon & Stephanie

I

SARAH

THE MOTHER OF PATIENCE

Stephanie Feger

S ome dreams feel totally and completely achievable; ones we can almost reach out and touch with a bit of determination, grit and planning. Your dream of buying a house could be feasible with the right financial planning and a commitment to budgeting. Your dream of moving up the corporate ladder could become a reality with proper education and on-site experience. Your dream to learn how to ski (or any other interesting hobby or activity) is feasible with lessons. Your dream to conquer a fear can happen with a willingness to do things scared. A dream within reach doesn't seem like a figment of our imagination; it's a possibility that needs a bit of fuel, a load of guts and your commitment to persevering even when the going gets tough.

Those types of dreams I'm totally and completely game for.

But not all dreams materialize with willpower and a hefty dose of "let's do this." Some dreams feel far, far away like fairytale stories that speak of princes in castles in places we think we'll never see face-to-face. These dreams can feel unattainable, fables even…

stories we tell ourselves that deep down we believe aren't possible anyway. These types of dreams are what we share in college admission essays. We hope it showcases to those who seemingly stand between our dreams and our reality a willingness to go for our aspirations. But deep down, if we're being honest, sometimes we feel swallowed up in an earthly reality that some dreams just aren't possible.

Or are they? A small voice deep within may whisper this consideration like a child who doesn't give up asking "why" questions (despite their parents' exhaustion with their persistence). Maybe the reason we don't write off a dream as false hope is because somewhere amid our unbelief lies a version of us that remembers what God said when He formed us in His image.

God saw all that he had made, and it was very good.
Genesis 1:31 (NIV)

Until it's good, God isn't done. We sing about it, but do we live it? We accept it as truth, but do we deep-to-our-core believe it? It's easy to dream when dreams materialize; it's a lot harder to keep dreaming when the one dream we want most doesn't seem possible. I know this longing, this desperate desire. And, I suspect you know it too.

⸻

I felt like a secret agent, being sly as I would drop the box into my shopping cart, careful no one saw my heart's desires. As the box slowly moved on the conveyor belt, inching toward the grocery store clerk who'd scan its barcode, I'd pray they wouldn't ask questions about its contents and my use of them. If my gaze avoided theirs, possibly I could make it to my car unscathed by the unknowns, holding my longest dream close so that no one could steal it from me. Even though, if I was being honest, I was worried it was already stolen.

At home in the dark depths of my under-the-sink cabinet, where creepy crawlies and desperate hopes lay hidden, so did the pregnancy tests, awaiting a day each month when I would see if my dream of being a mother would materialize. But my childhood dreams felt squashed month after month, and my feelings of excitement evolved into soul-breaking worries. Each step in my journey toward motherhood felt like an exhaustive walk of holding breaths, as if doing so would take away my fears and prepare me for an impending letdown.

The longest dream I ever had was one I know many women share: the dream of being a mother.

For many, it's an instinctual longing that we carry close to our hearts. We push baby dolls around in plastic strollers while pretending to feed and burp them. We watch women around us, taking subconscious inventory of the type of mother we will be from watching what other mothers do or don't do. We immerse ourselves in Hallmark movies portraying picture-perfect pregnancies with picture-perfect families experiencing life challenges in picture-perfect ways. Social media allows us to watch others live a filtered, picture-perfect world, where others are doing the things we dream of doing.

We yearn. We desire. We hope. We dream. And yet, our story isn't written like the pages of other people's books. Motherhood, and the path to it, isn't always straight. Many times, it's filled with detours, roundabouts, rocky spots and dead ends.

I LIVED THIS, AND SO DID SARAH

Abram and Nahor both married. The name of Abram's wife was Sarai, and the name of Nahor's wife was Milkah; she was the daughter of Haran, the father of both Milkah and

Iskah. Now Sarai was childless because she was not able to conceive.
Genesis 11:29-30 (NIV)

The first time we meet Sarah in the Bible, she is matter-of-factly described as a wife to Abraham, and she's barren. After the fall of Babel, we are taken through a lineage path that leads to Abraham (and eventually to Jesus), so at this point in Scripture, we are introduced to a couple who is about to endure one of the hardest things a couple can: pregnancy challenges.

When I study Scripture, I like to put myself into the context of the full story. I want to know culturally what was expected and what life was like, both of which give greater clarity to what we can learn about God through the experiences of broken people—and what broken women went through, Sarah included. Take a moment to put yourself in Sarah's shoes; walk her path with me. (And as we do, I suspect you may see some of your own life's path along the way.)

Sarah wasn't Sarah quite yet; God hadn't changed her name at this point. She was Sarai. It's believed that Sarah was beautiful, so much so that twice Abraham feared a ruler would kill him to have her as his own. Sarah lived in a time when a woman's identity wasn't defined the way ours is today—the scale of pounds and possessions weren't the deciding factor of a woman's worth, per se. Her ability to keep a lineage strong was, and it was made clear from the first time we learn of Sarah that she was struggling in that area.

Much has changed since the days of Sarah and Abraham. We have a plethora of shoe options, praise the Lord! I can't imagine all the walking they did without arch supports or strong hiking boots. Cars make transportation easier, and we don't have to worry about breaking in a horse when it's time to get from point A to point B. We live in stationary homes with more than someone in Sarah and Abraham's time could have ever dreamed possible. And yet, I can feel Sarah's pain. I can understand her worries. I can close my eyes and picture myself in her spot, feeling the daggers of stares from everyone around me for what I wanted so desperately to accomplish, and yet, time and time again, I couldn't.

Sarah didn't have pregnancy tests, but she still had expectations. She didn't have ovulation apps, but she was likely counting the days. She didn't have people offering advice from *What to Expect When You're Expecting*, but I'm confident she got her fair share of tips on what she should be doing to accomplish her purpose.

And that purpose was simple: She was supposed to have a baby. Period. End of story. That was her one job, and she wasn't delivering... literally.

Thousands and thousands of generations stand between Sarah and me, and yet, I know that expectation too. And I also know the feelings of inadequacy, of being let down, of disappointment, shame and guilt when, month after month, despite my dreams of motherhood, my body wasn't delivering on its end of the bargain. At the age of twelve, I received my scarlet letter in the shape of endometriosis. If Sarah had access to the medical equipment we now do, maybe she would have uncovered her scarlet letter then too. I had begun to accept that, like Sarah, I may not have been able to fulfill my number one dream of all dreams, being a mom.

If you've been a part of the church for any time, you're lucky to know the end of Sarah's story. For fear of oversimplifying, let me wrap her not-so-picture-perfect story into one sentence: Despite her pregnancy worries and fertility woes, at ninety years old, Sarah has a sweet baby boy, Isaac. Lucky for us, we are able to know the end of her story and not have to live in the beginning or middle. Hindsight is always a gift, right?

But that's not how we get to experience our own stories, and that's surely not how Sarah lived hers. She felt all the feelings. She questioned and doubted. She even laughed, and not the joyous kind. We know God delivered, but Sarah wasn't so sure He would.

No matter where you are on your motherhood journey—dreaming of what it will be like to be a mom one day, dreaming of the family you and your husband want to grow, dreaming of the day the test is positive, dreaming of a life where your desires feel heard or dreaming of a peace knowing God's working for your benefit despite your life's outcomes—Sarah's story has a lot to teach us about who our God is and why we should never waver in our faith and trust in Him.

SARAH'S IDENTITY CRISIS

It's likely no coincidence that Sarah is the most mentioned woman in the Bible.[1] Before God changed her name to Sarah, she went by Sarai, and in the New Testament, you can find a few references to Sarah. Whether she's called Sarah or Sarai, she is mentioned a total of sixty times throughout Scripture. That's no chump change. That's a lot of mentions, and we have much to learn from Sarah's story.

I see all the ways Sarah is referenced as a reminder of a deep identity crisis she must have been having. Not because of the spelling of her name (although I can only imagine how God gifting me a new name in my eighties would push me down an identity spiral), but because of her own motherhood journey, which begins in Genesis 11:30.

Every time I consider Sarah, I get stuck on the first time we meet her. When I find myself questioning a verse in Scripture, I've come to learn it's because God has more to tell me than meets the eye. So, I pulled out my Bible and Bible app[2] to review several translations of Genesis 11:30, the Scripture passage where we learn of Sarah's pregnancy woes for the first time.

Genesis 11:30:
Now Sarai was childless because she was not able to conceive (NIV).
But Sarai was unable to become pregnant and had no children (NLT).
Sarai was barren; she had no children (MSG).

At first, I was a bit peeved. Could she not have been given the opportunity to highlight her strengths before her weakness was front and center? Could Scripture not have told of her dedication to her husband and family prior to her body's failure? Would it not have been possible to have even added a little about her feelings on the matter? Anything else but the simple truth of her inability to conceive?

Even though the Bible doesn't speak of how Sarah felt in this moment, I'm sure all of us can fill in the adjective to this Mad Lib scenario. Sarah was barren and she felt [ADJECTIVE]. Inadequate. Frustrated. Depressed. Forgotten. Embarrassed. Heartbroken. Anxious. Desperate. Jealous. Isolated. Shameful. Angry. Stressed. Insecure. Like a failure.

All these feelings are valid and are ones Sarah surely felt. And yet, we are reminded of a woman's role during her time: to continue the family lineage. Other people probably defined Sarah through the lens of infertility (although they likely used other words than that one). The women in her community probably gossiped about her and her inability to do what every woman was expected to do. The whispers got hard to run from; she couldn't hide from the glares, the gossip, the judgment, even if she tried.

Her community knew her hardship, and the weight was heavy, I'm sure. And yet, Abraham (Abram at the time) went forth trusting and believing in God.

God made a covenant with Abraham in Genesis 12:2-3, declaring five "I will" promises and reinforcing the "blessing" He is offering five times as well.

> I will make you into a great nation, and I will bless you; I
> will make your name great, and you will be a blessing. I
> will bless those who bless you, and whoever curses you I
> will curse; and all peoples on earth will be blessed through
> you.
> Genesis 12:2-3 (NIV)

This covenant God made with Abraham has the potential to feel like a covenant He made only with him alone. But for this blessing to go through Abraham required Sarah, and a small detail was missing: She couldn't have kiddos! The way to the blessing was through Sarah, and yet, while Abraham went from town to town, following God's calling for him and accumulating wealth and status, Sarah followed. But likely not just with the luggage she helped to pack each time they moved.

She carried a heavier piece of baggage, the fact that month after month, she wasn't seeing the outcomes God promised.

While Abraham was able to redirect his sadness, Sarah was likely holding the babies of her friends and attending baby showers and birthday parties. She was wiping the snotty noses of other children, not her own kids. She was likely watching other women in her circles become mothers and make mistakes she secretly vowed never to make herself.

Jealousy began to grow, I'm sure. Fester even. Through clenched teeth, I'm sure she did her best to support the women around her, but behind closed doors, I can't imagine Sarah—the woman who laughed at God in Genesis 15 (and then lied about it)—kept her feelings to herself. She likely vented to Abraham (as I did to my husband) about the injustice she was living.

My journey to motherhood was a rocky path too, although not an eighty-nine-year journey, so I can celebrate that victory! After much trying, my husband and I did finally see a pregnancy test with a faint double line. I fell to the floor in awe of the miracle growing in my belly. God delivered. God heard my cries. I felt seen and loved. And yet, merely weeks later, I felt robbed of the relief I had briefly been given. What I thought was destined to be a picture-perfect pregnancy turned into a painful, unexpected and early in-home delivery of my daughter in my bathroom; an experience I don't wish on anyone.

The questions from loved ones on "When's the baby coming?" pivoted to utter and complete silence. Phones barely rang. No visitors arrived. A labor of love at forty weeks has a different outcome than a labor of love at ten weeks. Tears of joy were traded for tears of sadness. And, as I laid on the couch, numb to the world, the news scrolled with the current unspeakable story of the Casey Anthony Trial, a woman who was accused of murdering her daughter.

I had lost my daughter.
She had potentially killed hers.

I festered jealousy. I compounded anger. Layer upon layer, I found every reason to run from God instead of run to Him. I was next-level mad. And I was empty. Physically and emotionally.

In retrospect, I can see my own identity crisis alongside Sarah's. Who were we, two women with a purpose, if motherhood wasn't it? We were both empty and lost. And that's not a pleasant place to be; take it from my experience.

Sarah's identity had been created around her inability to have children. She was known as the woman who visited "the tent" each month, never with a nine-month reprieve to invite a bundle of joy into the world. She was Abraham's extra; his sidekick as he followed the Lord's calling for him. She went through the motions, but I'm confident she wasn't happy to do so.

The night that I lost my daughter, Faith, a miraculous shift happened within me after lying on the couch, disconnected from the world. My aunt called—the only other person I knew who had experienced a miscarriage—and proceeded to remind me of God's working in this horrible situation. It took her gentle yet focused encouragement coming from a place of understanding to lift me up and realize I was more.

And Sarah was too.

Just because our bodies have inadequacies doesn't mean *we* are inadequate.

In Genesis 13:1, Abraham followed the Lord's direction to move from Egypt to Negev, and Scripture notes he did so "with his wife and everything he had…" You could interpret that in various ways, but I'm comforted in the reminder that Sarah wasn't alone; she was Abraham's world. Together, with God by their side, anything was possible.

Sarah, a woman of great patience despite her challenges, is one of two women noted as heroes in the faith in Hebrews 11: "And by faith even Sarah, who was past childbearing age, was enabled to bear children because she considered him faithful who had made the promise" (Hebrews 11:11, NIV). The woman who was introduced with the identity of barren was later reintroduced as a woman of faith.

Now that's an identity to strive for.

THE THREE LAUGHS

We all have insecurities. For some of us, it's the imperfect bumps on the bridge of our noses or the shape of our silhouettes when we sneak a glance at our shadow. Some of us may be self-conscious of our inability to hold back our thoughts while others fret about our lack of professional progress. While I'll spare you the rant on my own insecurities, I can tell you that one I'm very aware of is my laugh.

I don't have one of those annoying laughs that make the walls shake when belted out or a squeaky one that is like nails on chalkboards. But I do have a laugh I'm highly aware of and always try to control. It's one of those that starts off healthy and happy, and as I get more excited, it pivots to my nasal cavity and lingers a tad too long. If you and I were to meet and I find myself in a laughing fit, you may not even notice my laugh insecurity, but as I read of the laughs spoken of in Genesis that align with Sarah's story, I'm highly aware of how cautious I would be to laugh in earshot of God, for several reasons of course.

You can't read Sarah's story in Genesis and not spend time considering the multiple times laughter is mentioned. Depending upon the translation of the Bible you have, laughter can be found in some form between twenty to forty times[3] throughout the whole Bible, and several times—three in particular—are found in Sarah's story.

As I studied the life of Sarah, praying for God to offer me insights into His loving nature through her story of redemption, I stumbled upon a beautiful sermon on Sarah shared by author Marian Jordan Ellis[4]. Among other insights, I was left energized (giggly even) on what we can learn from the laughter highlighted in her broken to beautiful story.

Do a quick Google search and you'll find oodles of articles highlighting why we laugh and the benefits of laughter to the mind, body and soul. But in Sarah's story, we get a chance to see three types of laughter in ways we likely haven't considered prior.

Laughter found in uncertainty and disbelief.
Laughter in the face of one's enemy.
Laughter in relishing the beautiful joy of God's promises.

The First Laugh

> "Where is your wife Sarah?" they asked him. "There, in the tent," he said. Then one of them said, "I will surely return to you about this time next year, and Sarah your wife will have a son." Now Sarah was listening at the entrance to the tent, which was behind him. Abraham and Sarah were already very old, and Sarah was past the age of childbearing. So Sarah laughed to herself as she thought, "After I am worn out and my lord is old, will I now have this pleasure?" Then the Lord said to Abraham, "Why did Sarah laugh and say, 'Will I really have a child, now that I am old?' Is anything too hard for the Lord? I will return to you at the

appointed time next year, and Sarah will have a son." Sarah
was afraid, so she lied and said, "I did not laugh." But he
said, "Yes, you did laugh."
Genesis 18:9-15 (NIV)

While in Genesis 17:17, Abraham laughed under his breath at
God's declaration that Sarah would have a child, Sarah lets out a
yeah-right-are-you-kidding-me laugh while listening in secret to
God's assurance of her forthcoming pregnancy in Genesis 18, and
God heard. Imagine looking God in the eye after He heard your
scoffing I-don't-believe-you laugh and lying to Him about it. Friend,
He knows all. Shouldn't we know better?!

But remember Sarah's despair. She truly didn't believe that what
God said would happen. She was old. She was tired. She had settled
into her identity of being Sarah the Childless, whether she liked it
or not. God had declared this promise time and time again, and it
was getting old, I'm sure. In the beginning, God's promise felt hope-
ful, maybe giving her some pepper to her stepper. But after a while,
her humanness got the best of her.

It's hard to believe what we don't see, even when God directly
tells us the best is yet to come.

I imagine Sarah's laugh here was a snarky one filled with pain and
disappointment. "Sure God," her laugh said. "I'll believe it when I
see it." Faith is anything but easy. We live in a world that wants to
touch what we believe. We want to see fruits from our labors. We get
energy from outcomes. We are a broken people, remember. Even
one of the faithful (even one of two women specifically noted as
heroes in the faith) was getting weary of believing without seeing
results, and I don't blame her one bit.

It's downright hard to believe a truth when we see everyone around
us experiencing what we desire without any movement to fulfill our

own dreams. Live a day in that level of despair and I promise you that your pity party of one will have an unwelcome guest knock on the door. Satan sees those party invitations and jumps at the chance to arrive, speaking lies in your ear to create false narratives pulling you away from God.

Have you experienced this type of laughter before? You hear of God's promises, but your life feels like a ton of broken or forgotten ones. Your father isn't the type of Father that God is, and you question if that type of Father really is out there. Your addiction isn't easy to let go of, or you've tried and you find yourself back at rock bottom after years of sobriety. You desire companionship, yet you can't find a man who is worthy of all that you are. You only find ones with baggage and piles of past mistakes, a lack of passion for the future and seeking earthly desires. You try month after month, year after year and the tests never show two lines.

I bet you've let out that sure-God-whatever-you-say laugh laced with a hint of "I'm not sure I believe you anymore." This type of laughter does no one a lick of good; you included. Good thing God heard that laugh but didn't listen to it. After calling Sarah out on her disgruntled response, God still delivered on His promise.

The Second Laugh

> God also said to Abraham, "As for Sarai your wife, you are
> no longer to call her Sarai; her name will be Sarah. I will
> bless her and will surely give you a son by her. I will bless her
> so that she will be the mother of nations; kings of peoples
> will come from her." Abraham fell facedown; he laughed
> and said to himself, "Will a son be born to a man a hundred
> years old? Will Sarah bear a child at the age of ninety?" And
> Abraham said to God, "If only Ishmael might live under
> your blessing!" Then God said, "Yes, but your wife Sarah
> will bear you a son, and you will call him Isaac. I will estab-
> lish my covenant with him as an everlasting covenant for his
> descendants after him. And as for Ishmael, I have heard you:
> I will surely bless him; I will make him fruitful and will

greatly increase his numbers. He will be the father of twelve rulers, and I will make him into a great nation. But my covenant I will establish with Isaac, whom Sarah will bear to you by this time next year." When he had finished speaking with Abraham, God went up from him.
Genesis 17:15-22 (NIV)

This laugh actually was referenced before the first laugh mentioned, but wasn't manifested until the birth of Isaac, whose name means *he laughs*. For years, I thought this was a direct correlation to the fact that Sarah laughed at the thought that her aged body could still deliver a child, but Marian Jordan Ellis brings forth a new consideration to ponder.

My husband co-leads a middle school small group at our church with a dear friend of ours. Unbeknownst to my son on his birthday, we coordinated a surprise party at our house with his small group. As I pulled into the garage, my husband, our other two children and a handful of his buddies waited patiently around the corner in our dining room to see his shock and awe at the realization that each individual paused their life to come celebrate him. It was magical in every sense of the word.

Eli's birthday is three days after Christmas, so our decorations were still up around the house and the unwrapped gifts were still under the tree. After we stuffed our bellies with penne noodles and my husband's homemade alfredo, myself and a few parents sat down for a "harmless" game of Ticket to Ride. I had never heard of the board game until that year, and it was quickly becoming one of our family's all-time favorites! Since it was a game of strategy all ages could enjoy, I was ready to kick butt and take names, and up until the last five or so minutes, I was.

The goal of the game is to rack up points by completing train routes. With a map of the United States as the board game's foundation, each player gets destination tickets and is charged with completing routes and accumulating as many points as possible before a player runs out of trains.

I was destined to be the winner until two people noticed my non-poker face. They could sense my excitement, and instead of focusing on their routes, they used their turns to put roadblocks on mine. A deliberate and risky strategy panned out for them, as I had points in my hand to deduct, taking me from the sure winner to the bottom of the winning hierarchy.

I didn't just lose; I really, *really* lost. And the two who conspired together to make it happen laughed.

It was a sinister laugh, like one you do in the face of your foes. It's the type of laugh that comes when you know your strategy won, and your enemy didn't see it coming. It's the laugh that God likely had knowing that Isaac wasn't just a promise to Sarah; he was a strategic part of the plan to build an army against Satan.

Isaac's name means *he laughs*, but what if that laugh is God laughing in the face of His enemy? That's powerful.

The Third Laugh

> Now the Lord was gracious to Sarah as he had said, and the Lord did for Sarah what he had promised. Sarah became pregnant and bore a son to Abraham in his old age, at the very time God had promised him. Abraham gave the name Isaac to the son Sarah bore him. When his son Isaac was eight days old, Abraham circumcised him, as God commanded him. Abraham was a hundred years old when his son Isaac was born to him. Sarah said, "God has brought me laughter, and everyone who hears about this will laugh with me." And she added, "Who would have said to Abraham that Sarah would nurse children? Yet I have borne him a son in his old age."
> Genesis 21:1-7 (NIV)

The first time I held Eli, my oldest, I laughed through tears like Sarah did when she held Isaac. After losing my first child, I held my breath through my pregnancy with Eli, afraid of hope being robbed again from me. I didn't realize I was holding my breath so long, though, until I held him for the first time, his beating heart against mine. I was complete.

Through Sarah's faithfulness during even the most trying of times, God delivered what He said He would: a divine promise. Her laughter isn't an I-don't-believe-you laughter this time. Instead, it's an I'm-glad-you-didn't-give-up-on-me-God grateful laughter. This is a joy-filled laughter at the sight of God doing what God does best, surprising us when we least expect it.

Maybe you've felt this type of laughter before?

Your day was chaotic and the school called because your child had a fever. How will you get it all done? God to the rescue. Unexpectedly, nearly all of your clients need to reschedule.

Thanks, God. You delivered.

You go to bed filled with worry. There are only so many hours in tomorrow, and you already have them claimed. Yet, your deadlines need more time, and there isn't any more to give. You wake up with a refreshed spirit (along with a blueprint of exactly what needs to be done, which you didn't have the night before).

Thanks, God. You delivered.

You are faced with an unbearable challenge, one you haven't a clue how to dig yourself out of. You feel hopeless and lost as to your next step. You go to your war room and open your Bible, unsure of what else you can do. The page you turn to and the verse that your eyes locked in on offers new wisdom. Your next step becomes clear.

Thanks, God. You delivered.

Each time He delivers, I find myself chuckling and saying, "Of course. Why wouldn't You?" This type of laughter becomes an expectant laughter. It doesn't mean that you know the outcome, but you realize we serve a God who delivers on His promises. Always.

THE DIVINE PROMISE

> For it is written that Abraham had two sons, one by the slave
> woman and the other by the free woman. His son by the
> slave woman was born according to the flesh, but his son by
> the free woman was born as the result of a divine promise.
> Galatians 4:22-23 (NIV)

I'm confident that God isn't bound to time like we are. I mean, we see our days as morning then night. In Genesis, we get a glimpse of God seeing days as evening then morning. He doesn't wear an Apple watch to track his heartbeat, steps taken or sleep patterns. He doesn't even wear the old watches that only tell time. Time, to God, just doesn't work like time does to us. And can I be frank with you? It's a tad annoying.

Out of all the traits I have, patience isn't one of them. I have a thousand things I want to do, and I'd like to have done them all yesterday. A business coach once challenged me to take my year plan and space it out over ten years. Great in concept; really hard for this overachieving go-getter. But I'm reminded that time is a gift, and *time* is not what is promised to us.

We aren't promised tomorrow. We aren't promised easy. Instead, the promises within Scripture are more like…

We are promised God's presence.
I will be with you; I will never leave you nor forsake you.
Hebrews 13:5 (NIV)

We are promised salvation.
For God so loved the world that he gave his one and only Son, that whoever believes in him shall not perish but have eternal life.
John 3:16 (NIV)

We are promised guidance.
Trust in the Lord with all your heart and lean not on your own

understanding; in all your ways submit to him, and he will make your paths straight.
Proverbs 3:5-6 (NIV)

We are promised forgiveness.
If we confess our sins, he is faithful and just and will forgive us our sins and purify us from all unrighteousness.
1 John 1:9 (NIV)

We are promised love.
For I am convinced that neither death nor life, neither angels nor demons, neither the present nor the future, nor any powers, neither height nor depth, nor anything else in all creation, will be able to separate us from the love of God that is in Christ Jesus our Lord.
Romans 8:38-39 (NIV)

Among all God's promises, never once does He add the caveat "in your time." Instead, it's implied and daily proven that God's promises are on God's timing. And God's timing isn't ours.

> But do not forget this one thing, dear friends: With the Lord, a day is like a thousand years, and a thousand years are like a day. The Lord is not slow in keeping his promise, as some understand slowness. Instead, he is patient with you, not wanting anyone to perish but everyone to come to repentance.
> 2 Peter 3:8-9 (NIV)

Sarah would have loved to be a young, energetic mother, I'm sure. But God had plans, and His timing was perfect. I would have loved to have held my first child, but God had plans, and I was able to hold Eli and his two siblings, Lyndi and Luke. You would likely have loved to have a baby, achieve a dream, accomplish a goal… add your own desire here. But we must always remember that God can read our story from front to back and back to front. He has hindsight already, and the waiting is purposeful.

God doesn't do pinky promises. He makes divine promises and those He never, ever breaks.

HE HEARS. HE CARES. HE LOVES. HE DELIVERS.

Sarah is my hero. She outlasted what I think my wits could. And through her path from brokenness to redemptive beauty, I'm reminded of three powerful truths about our God.

God doesn't make promises lightly.

If He promises something, He delivers. Multiple times in Sarah's story arc, God reminded Abraham of His covenant. Lucky for them, God's voice is audible; His promise clearly outlined. But for us, when we are still, we can hear His promises for our own lives. They don't always align with our wants and wishes, but they always are with our best interests at heart.

God can move mountains; friends, He's the one who made them.

Genesis 18:14 asks a powerful question we should hold close to our hearts: "Is anything too hard for the Lord?" The answer is clear: no. With one word, God creates. If His desire for us is our desire, it will happen—not in our timing, but in His. This is tough to grapple with because we tend to think we know best. But we don't. Not at all! Never forget God knows the full story—for us and for the world as a whole—and like Sarah, we are a part of a tapestry that matters.

God's timing is the right timing.

Our lives mirror the seasons of nature. In our cold, wintery wilderness, God is preparing. In the heat of the summer, God is working. In the sweatshirt weather of fall, God is reaping. In the promise of spring, God is planting. God is the one who knows what's best for us and when. And when the going gets tough, remember Sarah's eighty-nine-year wait. Her faith is a model for what ours should be.

Sarah isn't left in Scripture defined by her body's limitations. Instead, she is remembered for her persistent desire to see her dreams become reality. She may have faltered a time or two, but

God had a plan (as He does for you and me), and when Sarah gave up caring what the other women thought of her—moved past what her culture said her purpose was—and put her faith and trust in God, she was the one left laughing. A joyous, heart-full laugh of expectancy and assurance that God isn't done until it's good, and He has a pretty amazing track record of good.

Heavenly Father, help me see what I am capable of despite my earthly inadequacies. I am more than this body; I am Your daughter, and I trust in Your plans. Thank you for the reminder that I am not the keeper of time; You are. And what a gift it is to rest assured that You are keeping track so I don't have to. Please hear my heart's desires and offer me the reassurance that Your divine promises are the only promises that matter. In Jesus's name, Amen.

2

ḤAGAR
THE MOTHER WHO WAS SEEN

Shannon Carroll

It was one of those days, a day that every mother who has been a mother for more than seventy-two hours can relate to. I had two boys under the age of two, so you can only imagine what day-to-day life was actually like. I honestly have a hard time remembering a lot of the details and milestones of their first couple of years. However, this particularly hard day is still clear in my and my husband's memories.

David and I laid in bed sick with fevers of 101 to 102 degrees and climbing. Fevers are never fun, and when you have one, all you feel like doing is curling up in bed, closing your eyes and letting the world pass you by until you feel better.

Instead of laying down with the covers pulled over our heads like we preferred, both of us were sitting up in bed hearing the boys cry in their respective cribs, knowing they had needs and we didn't have matching energy. It was a horrible moment. David's succinct memory of this experience from sixteen years ago is, "It was rough."

We took turns getting out of bed to care for our young boys so the other could get some rest, but the reality was we both were up and down constantly, not getting much rest at all. It was life's unfair version of Whack a Mole—one issue, one need, one problem popping after another. And all we wanted was to be left alone to sleep.

If ever we felt at the end of our rope, this was it. Unfortunately, motherhood provides multiple opportunities for us to feel like this. I'm guessing you've probably vented more than once to someone that you've felt this way.

This particular idiom—"at the end of your rope"—literally means that we've reached a point of utter exhaustion or exasperation with no more patience, endurance or energy left.[1] Another similar idiom is "reached a boiling point." Or if we were British and could say it with a British accent, "at the end of your tether." It refers to an animal that's been tethered while grazing, but they've gone as far as the tether will reach and have run out of options and resources. Oh boy, I can definitely relate to feeling that my tether is tight and I'm at the very end of me. Can you?

Though we long for and fantasize about being mothers—believing it will fulfill our deepest callings and longings—we can all admit it's probably one of the hardest things we've ever encountered as well.

Motherhood stretches us; it requires immense sacrifice.

We have seasons of feeling alone to shoulder the burden, wondering if we'll ever have an adult conversation again. Sometimes we battle depression, longing for other activities to help us feel we have purpose.

For many reasons, I'm so glad God included Hagar in His redemptive story because she also battled these emotions alongside some terrible circumstances—yet God met her in such a beautiful way.

HAGAR'S STORY

Let's start with Hagar's name. I'm pretty sure you don't know someone in your circle named Hagar. We know that she originally came from Egypt; she was not Hebrew or a blood relative in this divine covenant-bearing family. Yet her name has Hebrew origins, and though it's a little ambiguous, it comes from root words meaning "to flee" or "flight" or "pressed into service."[2]

Names in the Bible give us clues into the person's character or life story. Hagar was taken from her ancestral home, was pressed into service to Abraham and Sarah and spent time fleeing in and out of the wilderness. Most likely, the patriarch secured Hagar as his wife's maid when they were traveling in Egypt. From the very beginning, we can surmise that Hagar didn't have a say in this life-altering decision. In fact, she isn't given a choice for several life-changing experiences. She's an outcast, a foreigner and must have been very lonely.

We don't know the details about Hagar's family of origin or what her life was like in Egypt. But quickly she found herself in the middle of some messy family dysfunction with her new owners. God had clearly promised that Abraham would be the father of many nations (Genesis 12:1-3). This is beautiful and exciting, but there's one problem—Abraham and Sarah are getting pretty old, and Sarah is barren. Even though God confirms this promise of a child over and over again to the chosen couple, they still allow room for doubt to creep in.

In her desperation to have a son and "help" God fulfill His promise to them, Sarah connives with a plan to produce an heir for Abraham. She craftily suggests that Abraham take Hagar as one of his other wives (a no-no in God's eyes) and have a child with her. In Sarah's mind, the child would be hers and Hagar would just be the "womb slave." In a moment of weakness and forgetting his amazing prior experiences of faith, Abraham sins and agrees to this outlandish plan.

He sleeps with Hagar, and she gets pregnant. We aren't given details about Hagar's feelings about the whole situation, but since we are women, we can make some educated guesses about how she must have felt. She had no voice. She had no option. She had no rights. We don't know her age, or if she was even a virgin. But Abraham (and Sarah) took advantage of her. I can't even imagine.

Let's pause for a moment and talk heart to heart. Today, one in four women is sexually abused before they reach the age of eighteen.[3] If this describes you, and what Hagar went through reminds you in some way of your story, then I just want to stop and hug you through these pages.

Hagar's story will resonate with you, and I pray that as we continue to walk through it, you can also feel the healing love and pursuit of Elroi, the God who Sees. It wasn't fair or right what happened to Hagar, and it wasn't fair or right what happened to you.

IN THE WILDERNESS

A few weeks later, Hagar confirms she's pregnant. As mothers, we likely remember that first moment. We know how our whole outlook on life changed when we realized we were carrying the miracle of another life inside of us. Even though Hagar had no rights to her child (even her womb was the property of her master), she—maybe for the first time—started to have a glimmer of pride and self-worth. She was going to be a mother!

Unfortunately, her excitement turned into a bad attitude toward her mistress, Sarah. Hagar finally had something that Sarah didn't, and she let Sarah know in no uncertain terms. The Scriptures say Sarah very quickly mourned her initial decision and complained to Abraham, "May the wrong done me be upon you. I gave my maid into your arms, but when she saw that she had conceived, I was despised in her sight" (Genesis 16:5, NASB).

Uh-oh, things are starting to heat up! But what did Abraham expect? Did he truly think this decision would end up working out with an abundance of rainbows and unicorns? Let's be honest—put a hormonal, pregnant woman and a jealous, barren woman together day after day, and there were bound to be fireworks (and not the good kind!). Especially when Hagar has felt abused and used for so long, but now she's feeling empowered. Especially when Sarah has longed for years for a child, and now she sees her husband's seed growing in her maid's womb. The drama was destined to get out of control. I can feel the tension rising from the words on the page.

Abraham washes his hands of the whole "girl drama" and tells Sarah to do whatever she wants to do. Unfortunately, Sarah decides to treat Hagar harshly. The word "harshly" in Genesis 16:6 literally means in Hebrew, "looking down, browbeating, to depress, afflict, humiliate." As women, we can read between the lines and guesstimate that Sarah gave Hagar continual verbal lashings. She put Hagar down any chance she could get. She made her life absolutely miserable.

Hagar had been taken from her homeland and forced into slavery. She was given, against her will, to her mistress's husband. And now she received continual verbal assaults. No wonder she did what her name implied and she fled.

We don't know how long God let Hagar run before He caught up with her, but we know when He entered the scene, Hagar was by a well on the way to Shur. She was running back home to Egypt. She was tired of this awful existence and ready to just be home. She hoped to never see her accusers or abusers again, so she was determined to put as many miles between them as possible.

We've all been in this wilderness, running from something or someone. Sick and tired of being sick and tired. Wanting to say goodbye to adulting and the demands of motherhood. Wishing to get out of financial traps and emotional discord. Dreaming of relief, a respite, a change.

It seems in marriages, in the context of inevitable conflict, God ends up putting a runner and a talk-til-it's-all-worked-out personality together. He has quite a sense of humor! I've definitely run away my fair share, although I'm more the talk-til-it's-all-worked-out type. Running can feel therapeutic. Whether it's running to the nearest store for some retail therapy or hitting up the ice cream shop to drown our sorrows in a chocolate-peanut butter double dip, we all have felt the need to escape from the troubles of life. Even the psalmist desired an escape when he penned the cry: "In the Lord I take refuge; how can you say to my soul, 'Flee as a bird to your mountain'" Psalm 11:1 (NASB).

Hagar ran and kept running. She was desperate and officially at the end of her rope. In her culture and time, she was basically worthless. A slave—a pregnant slave with no worth, no name, no fortune, no future.

And yet... God saw her.

In Genesis 16:7, Hagar is met by the angel of the Lord. Actually, she is the first person in Scripture to be visited by an angel! If it were my universe, I most likely wouldn't have chosen Hagar to be the recipient of the first angelic visitation. It seems that high honor should have been reserved for heroes such as Adam, Noah or Abraham. But here we see a major glimpse into the character and heart of our God. He loves the outcast. He not only knew Hagar, He cared for her. He pursued her! She wasn't sitting there pouring out her heart to Abraham's God with righteous prayers on her lips. She was fleeing, deserted, alone, nothing. And He came. What a powerful and comforting lesson for you and me.

This all-knowing angel of the Lord (Was this a pre-incarnate Christ appearance? Possibly!) knew her name, but referred to her with her position as Sarah's maid and then asked what she was doing and where she was going. Obviously, his goal was for her to confess out loud that she was fleeing and running from her responsibility and calling. Verse 8 in Genesis 16 (NASB) reads, "He said, 'Hagar, Sarai's maid, where have you come from and where are you going?' And she said, 'I am fleeing from the presence of my mistress Sarai.'"

The word "flee" means to suddenly bolt. Yep! I've wanted to bolt from the pressures and frustrations of life. Just recently, in a moment of doubt and defeat, I told my husband I needed to board a cruise ship and maybe not come home. Yes, that's overly dramatic. But I know you understand and have been there. Hagar didn't just think about getting out of Dodge, she acted on it. And she got caught by the angel of the Lord, who made her confess it out loud.

The first instruction of the angel of the Lord was that Hagar needed to return to her mistress and submit to Sarah's authority. And just as Hagar was about to argue with this crazy and unwelcome command, the angel of the Lord continued with a beautiful and life-changing promise. This is amazing!

> Then the angel of the Lord said to her, "Return to your mistress, and submit yourself to her authority." (But wait! There's more!)

> Moreover, the angel of the Lord said to her, "I will greatly multiply your descendants so that they will be too many to count." (But wait! There's even MORE!)

> The angel of the Lord said to her further, "Behold, you are with child, and you will bear a son; and you shall call his name Ishmael, because the Lord has given heed to your affliction. He will be a wild donkey of a man, his hand will be against everyone, and everyone's hand will be against him; and he will live to the east of all his brothers."
> Genesis 16:9-12 (NASB)

Somehow the command to return to the woman who emotionally wounded her was forgotten in this angelic and prophetic promise. And even though parts of this prophecy are hard to hear (not sure I'd want to hear my son is going to be a wild donkey of a man), Hagar receives what she has so deeply been missing for years—she is finally seen and heard, wanted, welcomed and given a future. The angel of the Lord is telling her that she has value and that the child growing in her womb is also valuable. She's not junk, and she won't give birth to junk. Just as she's heard the retelling of the promise to Abraham and his family, she's now included in the promise from God. She's one of the family. For someone who's been lonely and outcast for so long, this is truly refreshing news.

THE HOPE EFFECT

I've heard the effect of hope referred to as "hopium." Please forgive the reference, but it paints such a clear picture. Without hope, we have nothing to live for. We are defeated, in the dark and utterly discouraged. But one little glimmer of hope changes everything in our attitude! It is like a healing balm on a sore heart. Hopium gives us the courage to take the next hard step. It helps us move toward scary goals or fight for what is right. Hagar was given a dose of hopium by this angel of the Lord. Just the act of being seen completely changed her outlook.

Ishmael was named by God and his name means "God hears." Every time Hagar says her beloved son's name, she will be reminded of this incredible moment. God showed up on her scene and everything changed.

Her response is one of worship. Not only is she the first person in Scripture to have been visited by the angel of the Lord, but she is also the only person recorded in the Bible that named God! Listen to this!

> Then she called the name of the Lord who spoke to her,
> "You are a God who sees;" for she said, "Have I even

remained alive here after seeing Him?" Therefore the well was called Beer-lahai-roi.
Genesis 16:13-14a (NASB)

She had heard of Abraham and Sarah's God. I'm sure she had seen their rituals of worship and knew about their faith in this unseen God. But none of that was for her, or so she thought. She was just the womb slave, the outcast, used for what could benefit others.

But now she had her own, private encounter with God. He came for one such as her! Someone loved her and called her tenderly by name. What a gift.

She names God, *Elroi*, which means in Hebrew, "You, God, see me." The name of the well is translated, "The well of the living one who sees me."

Not only does God hear (which He declares through the meaning of Ishmael's name), but He also sees, *Elroi*. I'm not sure any additional words are needed as we meditate on those simple yet eternally profound meanings—for Hagar and for us.

As I'm writing this, a family we know is going through a scary time trying to obtain a diagnosis for their ailing daughter. They've walked through difficult hospital stays and ER visits with no answers. They've experienced terrifying symptoms with no known root cause. They've been tossed from doctor to doctor and pushed out when no easy answer could be found. (The "healthcare" system can be so frustrating!) Our community has rallied around this precious family as we watch this unsettling drama unfold.

Within the past couple of days, their local pediatrician and a remote doctor have taken a renewed interest in their situation and they've moved mountains to get her into a different medical facility. These new practitioners have an in-depth plan for more testing and they are being extremely thorough. The family finally feels *seen and heard*.

Even though some of the testing procedures will be rough and they still don't have clear-cut answers, they currently have a ton of peace and feel at ease. Why? Because someone is finally listening. Someone is intentionally showing they care and they're doing something about it.

This is how Hagar feels. Finally, she can breathe deeply because, even though her situation hasn't changed and she has to humbly trudge back and submit herself to Mrs. Difficult, she now has confidence and hope since God has heard her and God sees her. It changes everything!

I've often told my husband that my primary need is to be understood. (And I hate being misunderstood.) When I'm talking, I want him to listen attentively. When I'm hurting, I want him to empathize and at least attempt to understand. (Although we know trying to understand the woman's brain can be a bit of a daunting task for our men!) We all have a very deep need to be understood, and when that need is not met, we can get extremely frustrated—even to the point of fleeing, as Hagar did.

Hagar returns home (I'd love to know what that reunion was like!) and lives with this family for another fourteen years before we hear of her again. She gave birth to her promised child and got to be there to watch him grow up and mature. The tide turns at the fourteen-year mark when the chosen, prophesied and promised son, Isaac, was finally born to Abraham and Sarah. Five chapters later, in Genesis 21, we see another moment of drama unfold.

> The child (Isaac) grew and was weaned, and Abraham made a great feast on the day that Isaac was weaned. Now Sarah saw the son of Hagar the Egyptian, whom she had born to Abraham, mocking. Therefore she said to Abraham, "Drive out this maid and her son, for the son of this maid shall not be an heir with my son Isaac." The matter distressed Abraham greatly because of his son. But God said to Abraham, "Do not be distressed because of the lad and your maid; whatever Sarah tells you, listen to her, for through

Isaac your descendants shall be named. And of the son of the maid I will make a nation also, because he is your descendent." So Abraham arose early in the morning and took bread and a skin of water and gave them to Hagar, putting them on her shoulder, and gave her the boy, and sent her away. And she departed and wandered about in the wilderness of Beersheba.
Genesis 21:8-14 (NASB)

Sarah's original plan was for Hagar to be taken as Abraham's wife and their child would belong to Sarah. We see from this passage that those ideals never came to pass. Hagar, all of these years later, is still referred to as the maid and the Egyptian. She never obtained any other status within the family.

And momma-bear Sarah, when she saw Ishmael interacting with Isaac, her prized possession, threw a royal fit! Poor Abraham was stuck smack dab in the middle of these women and their sons and God's promises. God reassures Abraham that Isaac is still the chosen one, but He will also take care of Hagar. So Abraham sends Hagar and Ishmael away. I find it odd that a man of such extreme wealth such as Abraham only sent her with one jug of water and some bread.

We see later in Galatians 4:21-31 that one purpose of Hagar's life is to be an example to us of the futile nature of the law—and the war that happens between the flesh and the Spirit. Her offspring would become a great nation, the Arabs, but as was prophesied, they'll be in continual war with the children of Isaac, the nation of Israel. The conflict that started between these two women will continue for all of life on earth.

Even though Hagar is used in this situation and in the New Testament as an example of something we don't want, God still shows up for her! This is called grace.

Grace is getting what we don't deserve. God is the ultimate master of grace-giving, and we are the humble and grateful recipients of such amazing grace!

IN THE WILDERNESS—AGAIN

Hagar is sent away with few provisions (and again with no say in the matter), and she quickly becomes desperate again. Their water and food run out, and they feel close to death. You can hear the anguish in her momma heart as she cries out.

> "Do not let me see the boy die." And she sat opposite him,
> and lifted up her voice and wept.
> Genesis 21:16 (NASB)

After her last glorious experience in the wilderness where she met God and even named Him, she finds herself in the wilderness again, this time with her son and out of food and water. They figured they would die right here, even though God promised this wouldn't happen. (Remember, Ishmael was prophesied to become a great nation someday.)

I believe many of our wilderness experiences are actually crises of faith. When the going gets rough, our needs aren't being met, we don't feel seen or understood, we don't have answers, our children are suffering—will we *still trust* in God? Hagar forgot God's promises, but at least she cried out to Him in a raw prayer. She named God—but does she still believe He is the God who sees?

> God heard the lad crying; and the angel of God called to
> Hagar from heaven and said to her, "What is the matter with
> you, Hagar? Do not fear, for God has heard the voice of the
> lad where he is. Arise, lift up the lad, and hold him by the
> hand, for I will make a great nation of him." Then God
> opened her eyes and she saw a well of water; and she went
> and filled the skin with water and gave the lad a drink. God
> was with the lad, and he grew; and he lived in the wilderness

and became an archer. He lived in the wilderness of Paran, and his mother took a wife for him from the land of Egypt. Genesis 21:17-21 (NASB)

God made a way where there seemed to be no way. He responds to our cries and the cries of our children.

As a result of some ministry drama, our boys lost their best friends at church. It was absolutely heartbreaking to see their tears night after night and know they couldn't fully understand why their friends had left so suddenly. I couldn't fix their pain. All I knew to do was pray with them and encourage them to pray for new friends.

God heard their cry and a few months later, a sweet family with three teenage boys walked through the doors of our church for the first time. Their boys became fast friends with ours in a way that I knew only God could orchestrate. He hears our cries and our children's cries. Let's encourage them to also cry out to God for provision; training our children to pray and seek God is one of the best legacy actions we can take as parents.

Life went on for Hagar. Presumably, she finally made it back to her homeland of Egypt, since she secured a wife for Ishmael from that country. She may not have ever had the glorious, romantic story of being loved by another man for life. She may have spent her life never being truly loved. She definitely carried severe wounds from her past. She would be known throughout history as Sarah's maid and the "bondwoman" (Galatians).

But God saw her. God heard her cries in the wilderness. He met her right where she was. I'm so grateful for Hagar's life and the lessons she teaches us about motherhood.

GOD SEES ME

It was 2010, a super hard year for our family. With a one-year-old and two-year-old underfoot, we also had just delivered our stillborn baby at twenty-one weeks. The baby was so deformed that we were not even able to determine if it was a boy or a girl. We were crushed. My stepson had multiple appointments and needs during this hard season as well.

In addition, our house was on the market, and we were desperate to sell it in the aftermath of the horrible housing market crash. At the worst possible time, we'd get a call that we had to get the house in tip-top shape for a showing.

David had a fairly routine medical procedure that went south, causing him two to three months of recovery off work while in constant pain. I was working part-time as a nurse, we were still leading the church and I was attempting to manage and juggle all the plates, but they were starting to spin out of my control. It was too much.

I was exhausted. I was in a dark place—depressed even. Chronic stress and a lack of sleep will make any of us a bit more crazy than usual! I couldn't keep up, and I wasn't happy with my life.

I'll never forget the awful day when I was in the kitchen alone and the sharp knives caught my eye. I've always been a confident and fairly upbeat person, but the enemy knew how to creep into this vulnerable, tired, unmotivated and unhappy heart and attract me with demonic thoughts. I strongly considered picking up that knife and stabbing it into my heart to end all the pain in life. I was desperate. I was in the lowest of the low places. I couldn't take it anymore.

Praise the Lord for the Holy Spirit fighting against the enemy and smacking me upside the head for having that evil thought. I was able to turn away and reject the temptation. I don't think I confessed to David at that moment the specifics of what I had considered, but I did make him aware that I was spiraling out of control fast. He encouraged me to seek counseling, which I did. It helped.

I know what it's like to experience depression in motherhood. I know what it's like to believe the lies of the enemy that no one cares about and no one sees us. I understand how it feels to not have the energy to put one foot in front of the next and not be able to see how you're going to go on another day, hour or minute.

I want you to truly hear me—if God could meet Hagar in her wilderness, He can meet you and me in ours.

It might feel like no one else sees or hears or understands. *But He does.* He's waiting for us to just come to Him, lay it all down and rest at His feet.

When you are feeling the weight of discouragement, read this prayer from Psalm 139 out loud. Hear the precious Word of the Lord written for you!

O Lord, You have searched me and known me.
You know when I sit down and when I rise up;
You understand my thought from afar.
You scrutinize my path and my lying down,
And are intimately acquainted with all my ways.
Even before there is a word on my tongue,
Behold, O Lord, You know it all.
You have enclosed me behind and before,
And laid Your hand upon me.
Such knowledge is too wonderful for me;
It is too high, I cannot attain to it.
Psalm 139:1-6 (NASB)

Key words in this passage are *searched, known, know, understand, scrutinize, intimately acquainted, know, enclosed.* This is what a woman wants —to know that we are fully known, fully loved, fully secured. God is so good to offer us this hope and this promise.

God's promises can get us through discouragement. They can carry us through any defeat. They can break through any depression.

Hagar, a womb slave—one of the worst forms of slavery—was verbally and sexually abused. She was neglected and unwanted. Dismissed. Not included. But God still redeemed her situation. And He can redeem your situation and your broken heart as well, Sweet Momma. He specializes in taking whatever mess or shame or hurt we carry and making something beautiful. He redeems in a supernatural way that still boggles my mind!

My pastor husband encourages his congregation that when we are feeling down and discouraged and at the end of our rope, we need to open our Bibles to Romans 8, stand up and read the chapter out loud. Declaring these truths will break the chains we are carrying!

- Therefore there is now no condemnation for those who are in Christ Jesus. (v.1)
- And we know that God causes all things to work together for good to those who love God, to those who are called according to His purpose. (v.28)
- What then shall we say to these things? Since God is for us, who is against us? (v.31)
- But in all these things we overwhelmingly conquer through Him who loved us. (v.37)

Hagar and Ishmael were not inconvenient to God, and neither are you and your children. You matter. Your children matter to Him. If you'll let Him, He'll redeem your situation too. God is fighting for you. You might not see it all right now; so much of what God is doing is unseen. But you can trust Elroi, the God who Sees, in every single situation that's weighing on your heart.

GOD SEES YOU

I don't know exactly which season of motherhood you're in right now. Maybe you're facing hidden struggles of:

- Postpartum depression
- Exhaustion with the mundane

- Wondering what your purpose is
- Resenting your stay-at-home-mom status
- Resenting your working-mom status
- Missing your own mother
- The aftermath of trauma and breaking generational curses in your family
- Praying for your prodigal child
- Worrying about your children's future
- Loneliness and discouragement in your relationships
- Fighting fears of not being enough
- Overwhelm because you can't keep doing it all
- Dryness in your spiritual life

You wonder, "Will I ever emerge out of this wilderness?"

My friend, you need a moment just like Hagar experienced at the well of Beer-lahai-roi. Elroi, the God who sees you, is waiting. Claim His promises until hope emerges. The enemy can't win when we are standing on the promises of God.

―――――――

Heavenly Father, I'm in the wilderness, and I'm crying out to you. I'm desperate for you to hear and see me. I need a breakthrough. Thank you for the encouragement in Hagar's story that You care, You love, You can make a difference in my situation. I'm claiming Your promises and praying earnestly for an infusion of hope. In Jesus's name, Amen

3

JOCHEBED

THE MOTHER OF COURAGE

Shannon Carroll

"Joche-bed-head…" I've got to just get this out there before diving into the story of Moses's amazing mother, Jochebed. This is not a normal name in our culture today, and in Christian circles, we don't tend to talk much about the original, biblical woman named Jochebed. That's probably why her name sometimes strikes us as funny to say aloud and is challenging to pronounce.

Every time I told my husband I was getting ready to write this chapter on Jochebed, he'd respond by saying, "Joche-bed-head." It made me smile each time he said it (as I playfully punched him and told him to stop being silly). And now I'll never be able to look at my morning "bedhead" the same; I'm afraid it will always be called "Joche-bed-head" from now on. I'm sorry…. You're welcome. Ha!

That is probably a terrible introduction for a not-well-known mother who gave birth to and influenced three children who would change the course of history for God's people, the Israelites. From what we glean in the actual stories recounted in Scripture, she was so courageous and intuitive; she had faith that even landed her in Hebrews Hall of Faith. But we also know she had to be an incredible woman based on the unspoken fact that she raised three world-changers. I'm learning that when I see an accomplished, successful or faith-filled person, I need to start investigating his or her momma; most likely she was a special woman.

Jochebed's firstborn, Miriam, helped save Moses's life, watching over him in a basket floating in the Nile until the princess caught sight of him (Exodus 2:7). Later, Miriam became known as a prophetess among the Israelites. She was a leader of the women and publicly praised God for His deliverance (Exodus 15:20-21). Talk about a strong woman!

Jochebed also gave birth to Aaron, who would not only become the effective communicator and mouthpiece for Moses in front of Pharoah (Exodus 4:14-16), but he also became the first high priest. He was honored with the role that would point us to Christ, our High Priest! I'd say all of that is a big deal and would make any mother proud.

Finally, Jochebed was the mother of Moses, a special child chosen by God to deliver His people from slavery. Moses got to witness multiple miraculous acts of God. He had many encounters with the intense presence of the Lord Himself. And he was given the Law of God and the Ten Commandments, which have been passed down for thousands of years. In addition, he is credited as the author of the Torah, the first five books of the Bible. He was a world changer in every sense.

I'm sure you've heard the famous and true quote by William Ross Wallace: "The hand that rocks the cradle rules the world." This sentiment is true for all mothers, but Jochebed gets a triple gold star for her ultra-successful child-raising.

One of the things I love the most about Jochebed is her bold-faced faith in saving and raising Moses—even in a very evil culture. Conditions were not ripe for easy motherhood in her day. Hebrew babies were being killed by the Egyptians as they were being born.

Her radical acts of civil disobedience saved an entire race and nation. She exhibited the epitome of courageous motherhood.

In some small ways, maybe you and I can also relate to the conditions into which she was bringing children into the world. For many years of my boys' early childhood, I experienced a strong internal struggle with realizing what they were going to face in adulthood, based on the direction I saw our world heading. Fearing the future for our children is a common theme in the hearts of today's Christian mothers; if you've felt it, too, you're not alone.

My prayer is that the example of Jochebed will give each of us courage and a new resolve to launch world changers from our cradle.

THE BIBLICAL STORY OF JOCHEBED

As is the case with many of our biblical, female heroes of the faith, we don't have all of the details we'd like about Jochebed's life. But here is what we do know. She was a daughter of Levi, and according to Exodus 6:20, she married her nephew, Amram (although some translations insist they were actually cousins). Later, Moses, inspired by the Holy Spirit, would spell out in the law that these types of close family relationships were forbidden.

> Amram married his father's sister, Jochebed, and she bore
> him Aaron and Moses; and the length of Amram's life was
> one hundred and thirty-seven years.
> Exodus 6:20 (NASB)

What's notable about this verse is that Jochebed is mentioned by name, in a genealogy where the women were rarely spoken of. She was also highlighted in another genealogy in Numbers: "The name of Amram's wife was Jochebed, the daughter of Levi, who was born to Levi in Egypt; and she bore to Amram: Aaron and Moses and their sister Miriam" Numbers 26:59 (NASB).

Jochebed's name officially means, "Jehovah is glory." I love how biblical names reflect the character or actions of the person's life. In hindsight, we can see that Jochebed's life did bring much glory to God. What if we lived our entire life with the reminder and goal to offer glory to God with our every action, thought and word? What if that was the central goal of our motherhood journey—to see God get the glory?

The most famous Jochebed story is outlined in Exodus 2. Let's dig into this section verse by verse and see what the life and motherhood story of Jochebed can teach all of us.

> Now a man from the house of Levi went and married a daughter of Levi. The woman conceived and bore a son; and when she saw that he was beautiful, she hid him for three months.
> Exodus 2:1-2 (NASB)

Students of the Bible know that the space between verses can represent decades or sometimes even centuries. In between Amram marrying Jochebed and having Moses, we know that they had Miriam (most likely a teenager by that time) and Aaron.

Jochebed is not abnormal in thinking Moses was beautiful—all mothers think their babies are beautiful—but this word conveys a deeper meaning than what we all experience when we first lay eyes on our newborn infant. The word "beautiful" in this verse can be translated as "good, best, a good thing, precious, prosperity."

One of the first character qualities we see in Jochebed is that she has a discerning spirit. She knew that her son was special and set apart. Some theologians speculate that she had a vision about Moses's future calling as the deliverer of the Hebrew people. The text doesn't specify that, but we know something happened or something was communicated to Jochebed that her son was unusually beautiful or good.

I believe we mothers have an intuition about our children. We can sense the calling God has on their life. We often know them better than they know themselves, at least when they're younger. We know when they're up to no good and when they're lying to our faces. Thank God that Jochebed leaned into her discerning spirit; she didn't ignore what she felt in her core about Moses. It's this discernment that gave her the motivation to take radical action.

Don't downplay the nudges the Spirit gives you about your children.

When He presses upon you what to pray or how to pray for them—do it. When He gives you a Scripture or a promise for them—claim it. When He shows you a vision of what their future can hold—speak it over them. Utilize and maximize the spirit of discernment with your children; it's a gift that will provide direction for both you and them.

In this verse, we also see that she chose to obey God instead of man. We learn in Exodus that Pharaoh was worried about the increasing population and potential power of the Hebrew people, so he issued a mandate that all Hebrew male babies be killed (Exodus 1:16). It's interesting to note that godless leaders always default to being afraid of babies. The evil kings and cultures of the Old Testament celebrated infant sacrifices to their made-up gods, such as Molech. Herod ordered male babies to be slaughtered when he was attempting to prevent Jesus from rising to power as the wise men had predicted. Even today, evil governments promote, legalize and celebrate the killing of babies in the womb through abortion. It's an evil agenda that's been around for thousands of years. Truly, nothing is new under the sun.

Jochebed first sensed God's hand of anointing on her son. Then she recognized the current culture wasn't conducive for raising Moses in ideal and typical ways. So she hid him. For three months. I have no idea how she accomplished this and kept him from the prying eyes and ears of Egyptians or other snitches. A newborn baby is hard to miss—especially with middle-of-the-night screams (sometimes from the baby; sometimes from the mommy!). But she was determined to protect his life and even give her life for him. I'm sure the penalty if she was caught defying the Egyptians could have been as severe as death.

Today's culture may demand of Christian mommas a dose of civil disobedience. When man's law goes against God's law, we have an obligation to obey God rather than man (Acts 5:29). I don't have a crystal ball to see exactly where our world is going. But there might come a day when raising our children in the truth of God's Word becomes illegal. What will you do then? I pray our children see their mothers as respectful of our authorities, yet willing to do as Jochebed did and disobey when the world's mandates conflict with God's absolute, moral law.

I love this next verse in the story!

> But when she could hide him no longer, she got him a wicker
> basket and covered it over with tar and pitch. Then she put
> the child into it and set it among the reeds by the bank of
> the Nile.
> Exodus 2:3 (NASB)

On her own, Jochebed could no longer handle the situation. Moses was getting too big, too loud, too busy for her to continue to hide him. She recognized the situation was now bigger than she was, and she had to enact phase number two of this daring mission to save and preserve her son. I'm not convinced her idea of creating a papyrus chest and covering it with tar and pitch to send her son out into the Nile was her idea alone. I'm wondering if God planted the idea and gave her the courage to walk through with it.

Every step of her process is providing for the protection of her son and his legacy. She finds and creates a device that will hold him, and she ferments a liquid covering that will seal the gaps and further protect her son. Pause for a moment and picture her working on this DIY project feverishly in between nursing sessions and diaper changes. If she's anything like you or me, I imagine she's praying and crying her heart out to God as she brushes the tar and pitch thoroughly over the basket. Dreading the moment she has to activate the basket and send her son out into the Nile. Questioning if this bizarre plan will work. Grieving in advance.

Then comes the moment when she has to place Moses in the basket. This is a sacred moment of complete surrender, turning her son back to the Lord for His ultimate protection and guidance. Did she plan for Pharaoh's daughter to find the baby and raise him as her own? How much of the future was she banking on or how much was pure, radical faith and obedience in God's divine guidance? She pushed her son away from her, away from the safety of her embrace, away from all he had ever known. She pushed him into the Nile, a place where tradition says the Egyptians were drowning Hebrew babies, a vast unknown, a bridge to the other side—the enemy's side.

What would cause a mother to take such profound steps were it not faith?

She covered her child's basket in tar and pitch—much like we as mothers can cover our children in the Spirit and protection of God through our prayers. We recognize there are limitations to our covering and our ability to protect them on our own. Ultimately, they are in God's hands. But what a beautiful picture that we can cover our children through our prayers.

Another lesson we can learn from Jochebed is that she was a creative, outside-the-box thinker. I love seeing God provide and direct our steps in unusual ways; it's in those moments you know God is directly involved and making it all work out together for good. He utilized Jochebed's willingness to be creative and to go along with a potential solution that might not make logical sense.

I can learn from this. I tend to be a logical, reason-based thinker. If God presented me with this idea, I think I'd need a meeting with Him to hear how it was all going to work out. I'd need the roadmap, the reference manual and supporting evidence to get fully behind the plan. Well, hopefully by God's grace, I'd have the faith of Jochebed. But I admire how she was willing and capable to work with God in an out-of-the-box scenario.

Her immense faith challenges me. She went to extreme risks to carry out this plan. Her faith is recognized in the Hall of Faith chapter in Hebrews.

> By faith Moses, when he was born, was hidden for three
> months by his parents, because they saw he was a beautiful
> child; and they were not afraid of the king's edict.
> Hebrews 11:23 (NASB)

Amram and Jochebed exercised more faith than I can even imagine because they ultimately feared God more than they feared man. They were confident in their divine guidance—so much so that they didn't even question disobeying the evil king's orders. Their faith took them to the end of their ability and directly into the HIMpossible hand of Almighty God.

This is the kind of faith I want to have as a mother—to be so sure of my calling and my direction from the Lord that I don't waver when the world tells me I should raise my children differently. I don't want to be swayed by social pressure or social media. I want to stand firm and be willing to take big risks for the salvation of my children, just like Jochebed.

Her faith had an incredible impact on her children, as all three rose up to be great leaders of the faith. Moses is heralded in Hebrews 11 with six whole verses detailing his great moments of faith. I believe his faith was so strong, in part, because it was modeled by his parents. The greatest way to instill a healthy faith in our children is to live it out before them daily. They are watching, and our example does trickle down to multiple generations!

> His sister stood at a distance to find out what would happen to him. The daughter of Pharaoh came down to bathe at the Nile, with her maidens walking alongside the Nile; and she saw the basket among the reeds and sent her maid, and she brought it to her. When she opened it, she saw the child, and behold, the boy was crying. And she had pity on him and said "This is one of the Hebrews' children."
> Exodus 2:4-6 (NASB)

Jochebed intentionally sent her son right into the hands of Pharaoh's daughter and potential death. In wise preparation, Jochebed most likely planted Miriam in the scene to be available as needed. Her accurate anticipation ended up being a true divine appointment. My husband often says that he doesn't believe in coincidences, only in divine appointments. Even though Jochebed was an active participant in this scene, we know that it could only work out "this good" if the hand of God was also orchestrating every move, every timing, every response.

I pray for these kinds of divine appointments for my children. I pray that the Lord orchestrates their path in a way that only He can, knowing the future as well as the past. I pray He brings people along their path who can welcome them, mentor them, protect them and guide them in truth. The example of Jochebed inspires me to take action in prayer to provide the same divine experiences for my children.

She also is an example of allowing God the freedom to orchestrate it all. Remember when I said I'd like a formal meeting with God to work out all of the details ahead of time? Well, I also struggle with wanting to control every action involving my kids.

Stepping aside to let God move is an act of spiritual maturity by Jochebed.

I want to be more like this! He is way more capable and able to arrange every aspect of a scenario than I am with my limited and biased understanding. Jochebed completely let go and let God.

Then his sister said to Pharaoh's daughter, "Shall I go and call a nurse for you from the Hebrew women that she may nurse the child for you?" Pharaoh's daughter said to her, "Go ahead." So the girl went and called the child's mother. Then Pharaoh's daughter said to her, "Take this child away and nurse him for me and I will give you your wages." So the woman took the child and nursed him.
Exodus 2:7-9 (NASB)

Wow. This is a wild turn of events. I have some questions.

- Did Jochebed coach Miriam on what to offer as a solution for the princess?
- Or did Miriam just have an innate boldness and come up with this solution on the spot?
- Did the princess suspect that Jochebed was the child's mother?
- Why didn't she choose a wet nurse from inside the palace?
- Did Jochebed bring Moses to the palace occasionally while she was still nursing him, so he could interact with his new, adoptive family?
- How long did Jochebed nurse Moses?

Let's just say if I were Jochebed, I'd be nursing that baby for as many years as I could! Wouldn't you? Here's what I love about Jochebed in this situation—she was available for whatever role God gave her in her child's life. Mother, wet nurse, cheerleader from the sidelines… she was here for all of it and totally surrendered for God to use her however He chose.

As our children age, our roles as mothers change. No longer are they dependent on us for literal survival. They eventually learn to eat on their own and take a bath independently. Then they start reading on their own and some sad day, they take off driving in a car without us. We hand them over at the altar on their wedding day and wait for calls or texts with updates about their life. The transitions of motherhood can be hard for all of us. Adjusting to our role and the expectations of us is sometimes painful. There's a lot of letting go.

As Jochebed nursed her baby on borrowed time, I'm sure she savored each moment. I guarantee she spent hours training him in truth, instilling in him a love for his God and his people. She knew that eventually he'd be completely separated from her and raised by the world. This extra opportunity to love on and train him was priceless and a true gift. Instead of being mad at the Lord for taking her son away, I assume she had gratitude that he was still alive and she had been given a gift of additional time with him, especially during his formative years. I want to approach my motherhood journey with the same type of grace, gratitude and flexibility as Jochebed.

Never underestimate the power of influence a mother has over her children.

Jochebed's influence must have been almost palpable, considering how all three of her children were key players in the Exodus story. Our discerning spirit, courageous and bold faith, and willingness to allow God to direct our path will have an impact on our children. Yes, there are many wasted moments I wish I could take back as my boys were younger. Many times I blew it and would love a do-over.

Maybe you have those same feelings of shame and regret. I'm so grateful we serve a God who can redeem any of our shortcomings. He is bigger than any mess we make. His grace is sufficient, and His power is made perfect in my weakness (2 Corinthians 12:9). Take comfort, Sweet Momma, that God is enough. And it's never too late to ask forgiveness from our children, start praying for them and modeling faith. They are watching, even if they're not still living under our roof.

The finale to this dramatic tale ends with this,

> The child grew, and she brought him to Pharaoh's daughter and he became her son. And she named him, Moses, and said, "Because I drew him out of the water."
> Exodus 2:10 (NASB)

Once again, God asked Jochebed to surrender her son. This time she officially let go of his little hand for the last time, not certain when she'd see him again or what he would be like at their next encounter. I'm sure he was still young and impressionable. As any normal momma would, she would fear for his safety, protection and upbringing. In the dark of night, she would wonder what he was doing and if he missed her. A piece of her heart would be forever missing.

But she was steadfast, resolute in her mission to cooperate with God's plan for her beautiful, special, set-apart child. Because of her courage, her son changed the world forever.

HOW TO NAVIGATE UNCERTAIN AND TROUBLING TIMES AS A CHRISTIAN MOMMA

We see another glimpse of Moses's life in a New Testament sermon given by Stephen just before he was martyred. Stephen is chronicling the history of God's people, and he includes this nugget of a verse in the middle of his exhortation,

It was he (another Pharaoh in Egypt) who took shrewd
advantage of our race and mistreated our fathers so that
they would expose their infants and they would not survive.
It was at this time that Moses was born; and he was lovely in
the sight of God, and he was nurtured three months in his
father's home.

Acts 7:20 (NASB)

I want to highlight the phrase, "It was at this time." What time? Moses
was born in an era when the evil kings wanted him dead; they were
attempting to kill all the Hebrew male babies born at that time. This
king knew nothing about Joseph and the special connection the
Hebrews had to Pharaoh's house. He was evil. He plotted evil activities.
He had an evil agenda against God's chosen people. And yet, Moses was
born at this exact time. In a time when I'd imagine Hebrew mothers and
fathers were trying to avoid getting pregnant and bringing more slave
children into their horrific existence, Moses "happened" to be born.

God places our children in the specific and exact generation
where He wants them and plans to use them for His
purposes. Your children and my children are not born by
accident into a random era. No, we were all handpicked and
chosen "for such a time as this" (Esther 4:14).

I see a lot of moms (myself included) stressed about our world and
culture and struggling to know how to navigate it all. We're worried
about the future we're handing our children. If I'm being
completely honest, I used to be mad at God for putting me in this
time in history—not because I might have to suffer but because I
didn't want my boys to suffer or endure extreme difficulty or persecution. I wrestled with bringing them into the world at this time. I
had fears for their lives, safety and dreams. Can you also relate to
this source of anxiety?

I experienced an unexpected shift in this mentality when my husband walked our church through a full sermon series of Revelation. Somehow, God changed my heart through that in-depth study of the end times. I saw over and over and over again how God is in control of it all, and HE WINS! He is victorious! He cannot be defeated, no matter what. My fear and anxiety for my boys left me as I shifted my focus from defeatism to victory during that study. Do I still struggle with being sad over what they'll most likely face in their lifetime? Absolutely. What parent wouldn't? But I've changed my perspective from fear to preparation. I now see I have limited time to prepare them to be mighty warriors for God's kingdom, and I'm driven by that calling.

The mission overshadows the fear.

If Jochebed were here in person, I would love to hear her practical wisdom. I look forward to finding her in heaven (as I do all these amazing mothers) and letting her tell us the full story. But for now, I hope you'll allow me to share some tips from my own experiences. My prayer for us is that we'll emerge empowered and ready to approach the mission to which we've been called with boldness, courage and determination.

Just think for a moment. If you were the enemy, Satan, knowing you were eventually going to lose *and* knowing what a powerful force a believing momma is on the next generation—what would your attack strategy be for Christian moms? If you were trying to "take down" Christian moms, what would you do?

- Cause them to be distracted by social media, TV, movies, phones, screens and drama
- Tempt them to worry
- Make them feel like they're a failure as a parent
- Sprinkle in feelings of being overwhelmed
- Allow them to entertain thoughts of giving up

- Cause them to live a life of mismatched priorities
- Make them super busy
- Instigate contention within the family
- Tempt them to compare themselves with every other woman they meet

Has he been successful in getting you with any of these temptations? I know I've fallen prey to some of them.

A Christian mom is one of *the* most powerful forces on earth!

I feel like I need to repeat that louder for those in the back. **A Christian mom is one of the most powerful forces on earth!** Let's not underestimate the impact a Christian mom has as we devote ourselves to raising godly children, praying over them constantly for their entire lives. No one else has that kind of influence over our children. I'm so grateful for all those in my circle who pray regularly for my children. But I guarantee that no one prays for them and instructs them as much as I do.

You have a high calling. It's a higher calling than you ever imagined. God put your children with you for a reason, and praise God that He equips you to raise them for Him. Voices of failure, not good enough and comparison come straight from the enemy. It's time to take back the ground and rise up as empowered mommas—just like Jochebed.

We know we live in troubled times. It doesn't take very much investigation to see that our world currently looks a lot like the end times described in 2 Timothy 3:1-5 (NASB):

> But realize this, that in the last days difficult times will come. For men will be lovers of self, lovers of money, boastful, arrogant, revilers, disobedient to parents, ungrateful, unholy, unloving, irreconcilable, malicious gossips, without self-

control, brutal, haters of good, treacherous, reckless, conceited, lovers of pleasure rather than lovers of God, holding to a form of godliness, although they have denied its power. Avoid such men as these.

We can all agree that we are living in evil, wicked times. I pray and long for a Great Awakening or massive revival to sweep our community, nation and world. But I also don't believe our culture as a whole is going to take any steps to return to days of liberty and religious freedom. It's like being in labor. We are progressing, and the ball is rolling. There might be periods of respite, but I believe our world is careening faster and faster toward the Lord's return.

When we focus on the trouble and evil in our world, it's easy to get discouraged and wonder what the point is of being a Jochebed-type mom. We can so quickly become unsettled thinking about raising our kids in this evil generation. We have to turn to the Truth to find our encouragement.

> Therefore, since we have so great a cloud of witnesses surrounding us, let us also lay aside every encumbrance and the sin which so easily entangles us, and let us run with endurance the race that is set before us, fixing our eyes on Jesus, the author and perfector of our faith, who for the joy set before Him, endured the cross, despising the shame, and has sat down at the right hand of the throne of God. For consider Him, who has endured such hostility by sinners against Himself, so that you will not grow weary and lose heart.
> Hebrews 12:1-3 (NASB)

These verses should be taped on all our bathroom mirrors. Let's unpack these verses and see how they can inspire us in our pursuit of courageous motherhood.

"Since we have so great a cloud of witnesses..."

We need community for this journey. You and I need to be surrounded by examples of boldness and strong faith. Just like Jochebed's ancient story has spoken to us, we need current heroes of the faith to encourage us. Who are your friends? Who is in your circle? Hopefully, you are encircled by strong, courageous women. Choose wisely!

"...let us lay aside every encumbrance and the sin which so easily entangles us...."

Our own hearts can drag us down; we've got to get our hearts right first. We've already outlined several of the ways the enemy tries his hardest to trip us up. These need to be laid aside. Intentionally let go of whatever is holding you back from living courageously for the Lord. Pray and ask God to show you what sin or distraction might be keeping you from your mission.

"....and let us run with endurance the race that is set before us..."

This is probably my favorite phrase in this verse. I picture an Olympic race in my mind. The runner has run and run and run, giving her all out there on the track. Finally, she can see the finish line in front, coming closer into her view. She starts slowing down, slower, slower and slower because she's alllllllllmost there... slower... slower...

WAIT! This isn't right! That's not what the runner does! When she sees the finish line coming into view, she digs deeper into a different gear and speeds up her pace until *after* she crosses the finish line. The temptation when we get overwhelmed with the world and tired of the constant cultural battles coming against our kids is to slow down. I've had the wrong thought before, "Jesus is coming back soon, so why should I even keep trying?" Scripture is full of encouragement to run fast and faster—to not give up.

"...fixing our eyes on Jesus, who for the joy set before Him, endured the cross... and has sat down at the right hand of the throne of God..."

This is our solution when we're so exhausted from the fight. We look to Jesus and "fix our eyes" on Him. This means turning our focus away from the craziness and onto Jesus. It's a shift, a turning of our attitude, our thoughts and our perspective. It means spending time in His Word, thinking about Him and His truths, considering what He endured for our salvation. It changes everything.

Here's a word of encouragement for you—we don't have to do any of these things on our own or carry the weight of the world on our shoulders. Christ Jesus is our strength when we are weak. He carries us. He provides. He makes up the difference. He is enough. He does the work. Rest in those truths, Sweet Momma.

We press on in truth, knowing all of this craziness we and our kiddos are experiencing was prophesied and that we are encouraged to keep on running full force (don't slow down!) with Jesus as the prize we see at the finish line.

Truth adjusts our mindset and keeps us running strong with our high calling as Christian moms.

Inspired by the life and motherhood of Jochebed, here are a few practical tips to exercise our courage muscle and know better about how to navigate raising godly kids and grandkids in troubling times.

Pray for and speak life over our kids and grandkids.

I love to remind my boys what their names mean and use that as a way to speak life over them. My son Reid's name means "on fire for God"—and when I mention this and pray it over him, he's reminded of his ultimate purpose in this world (just like Jochebed means "Jehovah is glory").

Our job is to help prepare our kids to live strong for the Lord, knowing they will be in the cultural minority. I often pray over my boys that they will be "mighty warriors for His kingdom." They know they are being raised to be courageous warriors. When I drop my teenage son off for work at the local fast-food establishment, I remind him that I love him and always speak a prayer over him that he will "shine brightly for the Lord." Interestingly enough, that has become his reputation in this worldly environment—as a bright light! Praise God!

Praying for our children also reminds us of our role and God's role in raising our children. It's another avenue of continual surrender of our children into His hands. (Check out the chapter on Mary for a more in-depth discussion of this.)

Take your kids and grandkids to a Bible-preaching church.

Your kids need to see how God's design for the body of believers operates. They need to hear bold truth from the pulpit. This will help equip them to be a mighty warrior as an adult.

Get involved more in their education.

I'm so grateful we had the option to homeschool. This isn't for every family; each family has their own set of circumstances and needs in each season. Some government-influenced schools can become petri dishes of propaganda and indoctrination, so I encourage all parents to be aware of what their kids are learning and to have open discussions about it and what God's Word says.

Surround your kids and grandkids with good influences.

Watch their friends. Their friend circle is one of the greatest determining factors of which direction they'll take in life, and this influence includes video games, music and screens.

Read aloud with them.

My boys are in junior high and high school, and they still love to sit and listen to me read them books of great heroes of the faith. Subscribe to the free magazine from Voice of the Martyrs and read the age-appropriate stories with your children and grandchildren. I am normalizing persecution with our boys. I want them to know it's an expected and normal thing to be persecuted for your faith. When or if they ever experience persecution, I want them to know they are counted among millions of other believers who have gone through difficult times for their faith. I want them to call on stories they've heard their entire childhood about people who took courageous stands for their faith, regardless of the outcome, result or suffering involved.

Help your kids memorize Scripture.

There may come a day when our kids cannot readily access the Word of God. If they hide it in their hearts, it will come to their minds when they need it. We learned through my husband's amnesia season (detailed in our book *One Thing Remains*) that the Bible and its truths were the only things he didn't forget! The Word supernaturally transcends memory and lodges in our hearts and souls and lives forever. Any time you spend memorizing Scripture and helping your kids to also memorize it will have eternal value.

Reevaluate your busyness and priorities.

The rat race doesn't matter, Momma! I encourage you to get clear on what *does* matter in the long run. The time with our children and grandchildren is so fleeting; let's make the most of it.

Model a daily quiet time with the Lord.

Teach your children to love spending time with the Lord as they watch you doing the same thing. Family devotions, when possible, are also a key to training and equipping our children and grand-children.

Expose them to current events.

I don't want our children to suddenly be surprised at the evils in the world. We allow them to listen to some carefully chosen podcasts and channels that help expose them to what is happening in the real world. We have to be careful to not overwhelm them and cause too much stress. But a gentle exposure can be valuable.

We can all agree that there's immense trouble in our world—just like the world when Moses was born to Jochebed. It's possible we could be handing our kids a pretty tumultuous future. Please be encouraged and remember that our children are here on purpose for a purpose, and your influence can have a massive impact for all of eternity.

Heavenly Father, I find such comfort knowing that nothing is new under the sun and countless women have faced the joys and trials of raising kids in difficult and evil times. I confess the anxiety I've felt mothering my children in these uncertain days, fearing their future. That is not the attitude you've called me to have. Help me to have the courage of Jochebed, as well as the creativity and discernment she exuded. Help me to raise and mentor world-changers. Give me strength to prepare my children and grandchildren for what they may face, knowing you've put all of us here for such a time as this. In Jesus's name, Amen.

4

BATHSHEBA
THE MOTHER OF WISDOM

Stephanie Feger

"When I grow up, I want to be like Bathsheba."

My mom has heard me speak the "when I grow up" language before. When I wasn't much more than three feet tall, I would gaze at the grocery store bagger, proclaiming with passion I wanted to be like her one day. Whenever we'd take pets to the vet, I'd watch with anticipation as they cared for each animal. Later, I'd confidently state I wanted to be just like our vet when I grew up, too. And, time and time again, I've told my mom that even though my daughter is nearly three decades younger than me, her big heart inspires me. "I want to be like her when I grow up," I lovingly declare regularly.

We all have a "when I grow up" story, but I'm fairly confident most people don't include Bathsheba in their list of heroes, women they aspire to become or mothers they seek to glean insights from. And I'm pretty positive an "I want to be like Bathsheba" text is likely a text no mother expects to receive from their already grown-up daughter without a bit more context. I could almost see my mom shaking her head, confused by my written statement, through her follow-up text, "Hmmm… you're going to have to explain that one to me, Steph."

You and me both, I thought. Out of all the insights I expected to uncover about Bathsheba in my deep study of her in Scripture, wanting to model my parenting approach after hers wasn't on my expectation list, that's for sure. I mean, Bathsheba has a reputation, and aligning with it… Well, that isn't the type of reputation most would like to emulate. Am I right?

Bathsheba isn't the most popular woman in Scripture when it comes to public sentiment. Ask anyone who's been around church for a hot minute and they'll easily argue there are countless other women to glean biblical motherhood insights from. But Bathsheba? Like most of the community of her day, we all want to turn our eyes away even at her name, for fear her reputation will rub off on us like a sneeze actively passes around the "gift" of a virus. The "gifts" of adultery, child loss, becoming a widow, living a broken life. Those are "gifts" we'd love for Bathsheba to keep to herself. More flashy "gifts" like wisdom, patience and compassion, we'd prefer, please.

One Sunday morning, after my church worshiped together, our pastor, Kyle Idleman, walked onto the stage and began to pray prior to his sermon. Typically, I close my eyes during this time, like the rest of the Southeast Christian Church congregation, so I can hang onto every word he says and align my prayers accordingly.

But this morning, my eyes stayed fixed on the stage and the people moving around on it. As I listened to his prayer, I also watched the rest of the team assemble a large yet simple prop around the pastor for that day's sermon. Two long white tubes were carried on stage, and my grade-school excitement percolated when I thought our pastor could potentially engage in a double jump-rope act. (Listen, he's known to catch us all by surprise! Nothing is ever off the table.)

Instead, however, the stage team strategically connected the two tubes on each end and, in doing so, the tubes shifted their shape from linear to round, forming a perfect circle. As our pastor's notes stand was brought in, others began to prop the circle up a bit, to give it some depth. I was in awe of the simplistic art being designed within a few minutes of prayer.

Once he concluded his prayer, he made a quick pivot to acknowledge what I had watched be created and the rest of the congregation had opened their eyes to see for the first time. A white, semi-three-dimensional circle surrounded him, and all wondered why. The answer was simple, and yet not nearly as fun as the story my make-believe had been crafting. No double jump roping or circus act. Instead, he had created a visual sin circle, a reminder all of us—our pastor included—are sinners. He preached his whole sermon within the sin circle, challenging everyone in the room to see themselves in the circle too. As we read through Romans together, he humbly reminded us that not one of us is not a sinner. We all belong in the circle.

As he preached, I kept thinking of what it would have been like to be Bathsheba, the woman who is most known for David's greatest sin. The woman whom some suspect seduced David into adultery. The woman who was bathing on the roof. It was she who sinned first, right? The woman whose pregnancy was the beginning of a domino effect of sin. The woman whom others likely looked at in disgust, seeing her sin while she walked shamefully in the sin circle. The woman others likely gossiped about or pitied, declaring that they could never imagine being in her shoes. Or, maybe, the woman no one talked about at all… Or ever talked to.

That's the Bathsheba most people think they know. But I know a different Bathsheba… one I look up to.

One I can learn how to be a better mother because of. One who mourned for a sin she didn't commit. One who found herself deep in the middle of dysfunction and persevered through it. One who advocated for her son. One who experienced loss and didn't let it go without learning through it. One who was wise and raised the man who is known as the wisest king of all times. That's the woman I look up to. That's the Bathsheba I know. And that's the Bathsheba I want to introduce you to.

WHOSE SIN WAS IT?

We meet Bathsheba for the first time in Scripture in 2 Samuel 11, when her life and King David's cross paths. Now Bathsheba knew of David; he was her king for crying out loud. Her husband, Uriah, was one of David's best soldiers and was extremely loyal to the king, as noted later in the chapter. Bathsheba's dad, Eliam, is praised in 2 Samuel 23 as one of David's "mighty warriors," indicating that he was a soldier in David's army. So, Bathsheba's dad and husband weren't just members of David's kingdom, they fought alongside and with King David. There's no way she didn't know of him. However, David may not have known who she was. That is, not until he decided to not do what he normally would have.

> In the spring, at the time when kings go off to war, David
> sent Joab out with the king's men and the whole Israelite
> army. They destroyed the Ammonites and besieged Rabbah.
> But David remained in Jerusalem.
> 2 Samuel 11:1 (NIV)

It was customary, expected even, for the king to join his troops in war. But David was likely getting comfortable with victories and defeats at this point, as he had had many. He had people to do his work now. He no longer needed to muster up the courage alone to defeat the giants; he had help. So for one reason or another, he opted to bow out of this fight and let his people do the grunt work.

While they were fighting for David's kingdom, he took a long rest and didn't even get up until evening on the day that changed everything. No early rising for David; he took *his* time, enjoyed *his* life and opted for a leisurely stroll on *his* roof, a vantage point where *he* could see all of his kingdom.

This is a powerful "a-ha" moment that sets up when we meet Bathsheba but also changes her from the woman we assume she was to a woman who has a lot to teach us about ourselves.

> One evening David got up from his bed and walked around on the roof of the palace. From the roof he saw a woman bathing. The woman was very beautiful, and David sent someone to find out about her. The man said, "She is Bathsheba, the daughter of Eliam and the wife of Uriah the Hittite." Then David sent messengers to get her. She came to him, and he slept with her. (Now she was purifying herself from her monthly uncleanness.) Then she went back home. The woman conceived and sent word to David, saying, "I am pregnant."
> 2 Samuel 11:2-5 (NIV)

Have you ever played the telephone game? It's the one where you get a group of people in a circle, and one person whispers a sentence to another, charging that person to tell the same sentence (or at least as clearly as they remember it) to the next until everyone in the circle is told the sentence the first person whispered by the next person in line. Depending upon how many people are a part of the game, most times the beginning sentence muttered from the first person and the final sentence shared by the last person have little resemblance to one another. The sentence usually morphs, taking on its own life from the beginning to the end.

I feel like the opening credits on the story of Bathsheba are like a poorly played telephone game.

The amount of mix-up in very important details has created a likely false story of who Bathsheba was and how the downfall of David's sin began. Based on 2 Samuel 11:2-5, we learn the following truths, busting myths many Christians have believed for decades.

Who was on the roof?

Most think that Bathsheba was bathing on the roof, enticing David's gaze and seducing him. But when you reread 2 Samuel 11:2, it's clear that the roof being spoken of is David's, not Bathsheba's. Bathsheba could have been bathing in her bathroom, with the window open (or not!) but not in fear of being seen. Remember, the men were supposed to all be at war, and David should have been with them! Bathsheba could have been bathing in her backyard, but that was likely covered by a stone wall, protecting her from anyone walking the street seeing her. People on the ground couldn't see in, and very few had the perspective David did.

Who called for whom?

David was in a position of power. He was the king after all. Bathsheba was born into a family that respected the king, and she married a man who had the same sentiment. She likely looked up to him with the same awe and reverence Eliam and Uriah did. She likely took her bath, assuming privacy.

Then there was a knock on the door, messengers informing her that King David demanded to see her. I suspect she didn't question any of it; culturally it would have meant her death if she would have. She likely felt honored that the king the patriarchs of her home looked up to knew her name. Or maybe she was worried he would deliver news of her husband's death at war. Whatever the case, I can't imagine saying no to that demand was even allowed. Bathsheba didn't call for David; it was the other way around.

Who slept with whom?

If I've come to learn anything about the Word, it's this: every single word in the Word matters. The context, the order, what is written and what is left out, all of it tells the story in the way God wants it told. Little is spoken about what happened between the time David called for Bathsheba and when the sinful act happened, but Scripture notes "She came to him, and he slept with her." David used his power to accomplish what he desired, and what he desired was to sleep with Bathsheba, one of his soldier's wives. Many see this scenario as likely rape, where a man abuses his power to accomplish what he desires.

If you sit with this Scripture passage, you'll uncover she wasn't on the roof, she didn't call for David and she didn't choose to sleep with him. She was handed a bad situation, and because she lived thousands of years before the #MeToo movement, she likely carried the weight of it all alone.

I can feel Bathsheba's pain. As I read her story, I'm transported to my fifteen-year-old self, working my first job as a traveling actress playing Lydia the Lobster in a cheesy outdoor play for YMCA summer camps. In my red leotard and fluffy tutu and wearing two red oven mitts for lobster claws, I experienced my first claim to fame as a stage actress.

It was also my first of several feelings of shame from being the victim of another person's sin. At the end of the summer when my seasonal job ended, the theater team hosted an arts experience for all the YMCA summer camp kids. During this day, artists of all types came to a park where they could share their gifts with the YMCA children.

One musician who was part of a band chose to position himself on a picnic bench in such a way as to expose himself to me in broad daylight. Locking eyes with me when I came to check on his band— my tasked job for the day—he knew what he did, and it brought him satisfaction. I, on the other hand, was reprimanded by my boss since I told one of my friends in the theater crew first and not her. No care was taken to ensure I was okay. And I promise you, twenty-five years later, I'm still not.

I can feel Bathsheba's shame. Her story takes me back to my first and only time that a driver's education instructor picked me up from school to teach me the rules of the road. During a time when cell phones were nonexistent and the world's eyes weren't quite open to how people in power abused these one-on-one situations, I was alone with a man who took advantage of our professional time together and created lasting scars in my life. His inappropriate words about me and other women confused me. His demand for me to drive slower behind girls running in the park so he could inappropriately watch them left me speechless. His touching of my exposed leg while I drove the vehicle on the interstate immobilized me. And his manipulative plan to get inside my home, where I was alone, broke me.

While I feel lucky to have made it through the situation without being raped, I know others weren't. And, the hardest part of the whole situation was the cops chose his side, not mine. He was a business owner. I was just a little girl.

I can feel Bathsheba's mourning. By the time I had my third job out of college, I figured all this power stuff was behind me. I could focus on my work and build the life I wanted to. My skill, work ethic and passion would propel me up the corporate ladder. But, yet again, a man in the organization I worked for began saying inappropriate comments to me and inappropriately tickling me without my consent during work. I was in a committed relationship. I showed no signs of interest outside of friendship. He was decades older than I was. He crossed a line, but after I told my boss, I was reminded I should do nothing to solicit this type of behavior. I had done nothing to get it in the first place, and yet, I was the one charged with not letting it continue.

I feel the weight Bathsheba carried alone—that of embarrassment, guilt, shame and worry. I can imagine she felt extremely violated and yet also afraid, unsure of what to do next, especially when she learned of her pregnancy and what that usually meant for women in her situation. Not only was she pregnant by someone other than her husband, but that child was the king's. She could have lost her life over that fact.

Instead, she was brave and courageous. She looked fear in the eyes and, despite the outcomes of the sin she was the victim of, spoke truth. "I am pregnant" is the first of the few words we see in Scripture spoken from the lips of Bathsheba. The woman who could have run, shamed by a situation she didn't want, chose to stay, no matter the consequences. That's a woman—a mother—worthy of grace.

YOUR PAST DOESN'T DEFINE YOU; GOD DOES. AND, LUCKY FOR US, HE REDEEMS US.

Second Samuel 11 continues to tell the story of David's actions following this news. While likely unexpected news to David, I'm sure Bathsheba wasn't surprised. Scripture tells us that she was bathing because she was partaking in a purifying ritual that women did after their menstrual cycles. So she was probably extremely fertile at the time David called for her. Expected or not, her truth became his truth too. What he did with it, well… It's a story laced with sadness, showing what sin does to us if we let it.

A lie may start out as a small white lie, one seemingly unimportant and meant to not cause harm. But what happens when that white lie evolves? What was meant as something harmless can turn into something major quickly. Lies snowball, and so does sin.

It does for us, and it did for David. Instead of owning his truth—that he slept with a married woman and got her pregnant—he wanted to find a way to dig a grave and bury it. But in his attempt to bury the sin, the outcome was the burial of Bathsheba's husband. David planned to get Uriah to sleep with his wife. But Uriah was loyal to the king and refused to have a benefit that his men didn't have. David's cover-up plan didn't work. He positioned Uriah for death in war and made Uriah hand-deliver the note to the field commander.

> In the morning David wrote a letter to Joab and sent it with Uriah. In it he wrote, "Put Uriah out in front where the fighting is fiercest. Then withdraw from him so he will be struck down and die." So while Joab had the city under

siege, he put Uriah at a place where he knew the strongest defenders were. When the men of the city came out and fought against Joab, some of the men in David's army fell; moreover, Uriah the Hittite died.

2 Samuel 11:14-17 (NIV)

Sin isn't a one-and-done experience. It's like the effects sugar has on our bodies. We can't just eat one piece of candy. Our body craves more, subconsciously telling us we need it. Sin is the same in that sense. When we sin without seeking forgiveness, the sin has the power to multiply. It whispers in your ear that no one will know, and it grows. Before you know it, sin can become larger than you ever dreamed it could be. And David's sin story is proof of it. Had he just gone with his soldiers to war, Bathsheba may have had a different story herself, one that didn't have David's sin attached to it.

One choice can be that deciding factor. One choice can also be the shift of turning away from sin and toward God. David made a choice to lie. Bathsheba made a choice to speak the truth.

Two sides of a joined coin, but God saw their stories differently. And, per God's usual, He chose to use this brokenness for purpose.

Bathsheba mourned for her husband, Uriah, after hearing of his death. The Bible notes that: "After the time of mourning was over, David had her brought to his house, and she became his wife and bore him a son. But the thing David had done displeased the Lord" (2 Samuel 11:27, NIV).

God likely mourned with her and mourned knowing that her first son born with David wouldn't survive as a consequence of David's sin. God carried her sadness and grief along with her as she lost her husband and her son, two losses too much for this loyal woman. But God knew the end of her story, one where tears would be wiped and wisdom found in their place. God loved her and would love her secondborn, Solomon.

God wasn't displeased with Bathsheba. He was displeased with David. It wasn't Bathsheba's actions that were the problem; it was David's. As we learn more about Bathsheba's story—both what is spoken and what isn't—we can see clearly that God doesn't define you by your past. David's past deepened his faith, reliance and relationship with God. And Bathsheba's past played a pivotal role in God's larger plan; the plan that brought forth our Redeemer.

HER SILENCE SPOKE VOLUMES

Bathsheba appears to be a woman of few words. In Scripture, we hear her speak her unwanted truth—"I am pregnant"—in 2 Samuel 11. But after that, we don't hear her own words again until 1 Kings 1. Life happened in the in-between. She's actively raising a son who will become a wise king during that time.

I'm reminded of a poem I heard of years ago, *The Dash* by Linda Ellis[1]. Her poem discusses a man who spoke at the funeral of a friend and referenced the fact that a tombstone only highlights two dates: the date you're born and the date you die. The dash—the line connecting those two dates—is actually what matters most. It's where life happens.

From when we learn of Bathsheba and the beginning of her hardship to when she resurfaces to stand up for her son, Solomon, she is living her dash. That quiet time is anything but quiet. I suspect she's doing a lot more than anyone around her knows. For she's raising a son who is destined to be king. She's mothering in the shadows, with trauma following her day in and day out. She's raising the son of a man who stole her life and husband from her and forced her to live another life. She did hard things, and she did it for God and for her son.

Whether we are aware of it or not, our past doesn't have to define us, but it does shape us.

We choose situations based on our experiences and those outcomes. We try to not repeat past mistakes, and our growth happens because of hardships, and sometimes despite them.

I am highly aware I'm raising a daughter who has her eyes opened to the beauty God surrounds us with as well as the sin that exists among us. I don't want her story to include chapters in it like my past did.

I am raising two boys who I want to stand up for what's right when they see wrong in their path. I want them to be men of honor, not men who steal it. I am raising children I hope God will be proud of, and through open, honest and vulnerable conversations, I'm laying a foundation fertilized by my past traumas with the goal of shielding them from similar ones.

I've heard people say that hurt people hurt people. I've actually been on the receiving side of that statement. And, if I'm being honest, I've also been the one to do the hurting. But I'd like to flip that statement to note that hurting mothers have the power to break the cycle. And that's the path Bathsheba took. It's evident as you read the pages in 2 Samuel after Bathsheba's arrival. Her pain went deep, and after Solomon was born, she knew her task: to raise a man worthy of God's plan. She stepped aside but didn't step away. Instead, she stepped up. In the quiets of the story, Bathsheba was mothering a son in a way the other wives of David didn't.

During this time, David's son, Amnon, was falling in love with his sister, Tamar. He was so in love that he made himself sick while concocting a plan that would lead to him raping her. (Sounds familiar, huh?) His brother, Absalom, was so upset with Amnon's act that he ordered his men to kill his brother. (Again… the apple isn't falling far!) While Solomon was absorbing Bathsheba's wisdom, his half-brothers were falling into the same sinful, broken pattern of their father.

"Do as I say, not as I do" was David's parenting approach. But Bathsheba made a pivot, showing Solomon how to act by behaving how God would want her to. That, my friends, is a mother we should strive to be like. She did not require the limelight; instead, she knew where her greatest power lay—in her dash, in the years spent parenting Solomon.

HER WISDOM BORE WISDOM

David's son Absalom, who killed his brother Amnon, wanted to be king, so much so that he conspired against his father to get the title. He acquired popularity and status and threatened David so much that he fled. But soon, through a serendipitous series of events, Absalom passed, and that fear diminished.

We open 1 Kings to this statement: *When King David was very old...* A long time has passed, although it's not known the exact number of years. Scholars suspect Solomon was likely in his twenties, though. At this time, David's son Adonijah, born next after Absalom, began making moves without his father's knowledge to become king.

Bathsheba reappears in the story and is quick to gracefully stand up for her son to King David. The prophet Nathan makes Bathsheba aware of Adonijah's intentions and encourages her to speak with David, and she does. This is the first time we hear her words after her pregnancy announcement in 2 Samuel.

> She said to him, "My lord, you yourself swore to me your servant by the Lord your God: 'Solomon your son shall be king after me, and he will sit on my throne.' But now Adonijah has become king, and you, my lord the king, do not know about it. He has sacrificed great numbers of cattle, fattened calves, and sheep, and has invited all the king's sons, Abiathar the priest and Joab the commander of the army, but he has not invited Solomon your servant. My lord the

king, the eyes of all Israel are on you, to learn from you who
will sit on the throne of my lord the king after him. Otherwise, as soon as my lord the king is laid to rest with his ances-
tors, I and my son Solomon will be treated as criminals."
1 Kings 1:17-21 (NIV)

I suspect Bathsheba was a force to be reckoned with. She was probably
a woman of little words but when she spoke, she did so with precision
and purpose. I envision her as someone who was able to beautifully
embody the nurturing parts of her feminine design while also having a
courage that very few women of her time possibly had. If I lived
during her time, I think we'd have a lot in common; I would have
wanted to be one of her besties. And I suspect she'd be that friend who
would encourage you to do hard things when they mattered and
embrace silence when words spoken wouldn't move mountains.

I've learned how to do hard things. Keeping my words close when
they don't move mountains... that's an area I can strengthen. Hard
things, though, I've got that covered. And much like Bathsheba, I'm
ready to use my voice to stand up for my children when and where
they need me.

A few months before the pandemic swept over the world, heartbreak
swept over my world. My youngest child began experiencing hardships that I just couldn't prevent. When he was little, I could hold
him tight, kiss his boo-boos and take away his pains. But preschool
offered a new set of challenges for my sweet, sensory-seeking
blondie. He could do so many things well beyond his few short
years, but he couldn't sit in the square on the carpet when asked. He
had a spark for life, but that spark was being diminished each day
when he would be told by his teachers of his faults, not his strengths.

I knew things had gone too far when he began telling me he wasn't
a good boy. Of course, he was, despite his sometimes inappropriate
childish actions. Goodness, I taught him, wasn't something you
earned. It was something you were made from. I attempted to talk
to the principal and his teachers, but no amount of discussion

changed things. My little light was growing dark. And I needed to act.

One day on the way to school, I had an epiphany. What if we shifted how we saw ourselves by focusing on what we could control and letting go of what we couldn't? I was doing that in my own entrepreneurial life as a grown woman navigating personal and professional challenges daily. Surely the same approach could work for him. And thus our family's motto was born.

I am good.
God loves me.
I can do good things.

I started by reminding him and his siblings of what God said when He made us. He only makes good things, us included. God's love is endless, I reminded him. He loves you no matter what you do. Both of those truths should always come before anything else. And because we are good, we have the power to do good. That's where I reminded my little guy of his ability in his story: He can make daily choices, and good can be on the menu.

While Bathsheba may not have cross-stitched a family motto for her and Solomon to live by, she likely was a walking family motto. Wisdom bears wisdom.

Every situation she faced—the ones we know of and those we don't —gave her the opportunity to learn. She gained wisdom by walking a life filled with hardship, shame, guilt, frustration, sadness and heartbreak. But through it, she raised a son who knew how to lead because wisdom was his foundation. Much like my son, who still to this day can recite our family motto, Solomon knew his inherent goodness, knew God loved him and knew he was destined to do good things.

BATHSHEBA WAS A PART OF GOD'S REDEMPTION STORY. AND, SO ARE YOU.

God knows sin exists. He is highly aware of its goal to derail us, its power to break us. God knows, though, that through Him anything is possible, and just like a mother with her child, God never gives up on us. Instead, He uses our situations for purpose.

God turns chaos into order.

From the first chapter of the Bible, God began to make order out of what was likely a chaotic creation situation. He saw chaos after the Fall through Noah's time and pressed the reset button, but in a way that had our best interest at heart. God saw the chaos David's sin created in Bathsheba's life, but He created order there, too, leaving her as one of the five women mentioned in the genealogy of Jesus in Matthew 1. Bathsheba, a woman with a broken past, is a part of the lineage of our Savior. If God can make order from her chaos, I bet He can do so with yours.

You were chosen for your child on purpose and with purpose.

Ever wondered what sort of game God was playing when He chose you to be your child's mother? Many times I question if I'm strong enough for the task. But I'm reminded that God knows exactly what our children need. And, guess what? It's us. He knows our past dysfunction and believes that our wisdom from it and through it will shape the next generation just how God wants us to if we bring Him in for the journey. Bathsheba didn't make it through any aspect of her life alone, and neither can you.

God expects you to be your child's advocate.

Because Bathsheba stood up for Solomon, he was given the title of king and was able to continue the path God had planned. But that path required a strong momma to have the courage to stand up for what she knew was right and who she knew needed it most. We know our children. We know what they need and what they deserve. Sometimes, they find themselves in situations where they are voiceless or they need another voice to advocate for them. Psst… that other voice can and should be you. But choose to use your voice like Bathsheba did. Her voice was filled with respect and truth. Both are needed to follow God's path.

Motherhood, I've come to learn, is a journey with loads of twists and turns. It, alone, is challenging, but when you have trauma in your past or dysfunction in the rearview mirror, it's hard to keep your hands on the wheel. Sometimes, you'll pull out the Carrie Underwood request, begging for Jesus to take the wheel entirely. But rest assured that God has confidence in you, Momma. He chose you for a reason. He knows your past and He wants to help carry the load as you break generational trauma. You aren't in the business of passing that on. Instead, you're charged with passing on wisdom.

Heavenly Father, hold close my past pains and traumas that have impacted how I see the world, how I see myself. Help me to see me through Your eyes; help me see the strong, capable, worthy woman and mother you made me to be. Remind me daily that I am good, You love me and I have the power to do good things with you by my side. Help me, Lord, to not define myself by the world's definition but rather by yours. In Jesus's name, Amen.

5

THE SHUNAMMITE WOMAN
THE MOTHER OF CONTENTMENT

Stephanie Feger

I had indeed experienced the feelings before, in another chapter of my life and under different circumstances. But their familiarity served as undeniable proof we had not been strangers; I had once allowed them in the front door when they knocked. And yet again, they stood before me, knocking once more.

At fifteen years old, the emotions showed up unannounced and unwelcomed, like an uninvited houseguest; one that I wasn't allowed to kick out no matter how much I wanted to. (And believe me, I tried!) As I sat in my mom's car hearing the news that she and my dad were getting a divorce, I was immobilized. Although the situation was amicable, my world crumbled.

In my early thirties, the feelings appeared yet again, when the climb to success left me withered and depleted. I told my husband if that is what success felt like, I wanted none of it. Easier said than done, however, and I continued robotically moving through the motions even though I felt merely a shell of the person I was called to be.

My exterior appeared polished and pieced together, but the woman on the inside was falling apart.

This spot of despair is not a place you want to find yourself. It's the pits, literally. And a few years into owning my own business, I found myself there, yet again, in the same uncomfortable spot. This time, however, the shovel built from earthly coping skills I had used in the past to dig myself out of the depths of discouragement wasn't sturdy enough anymore. The handle must have broken from all the years I had overused what just got me by. Situational depression had become a lost puppy following me throughout life, but this time the puppy had aged, growing in size and weight, and was on top of me, weighing me down. This time was different.

> It was when I sat in my closet that day, experiencing my lowest of lows, where God placed a very simple message on my heart. *Stephanie, it's time to ask for help.*

Isn't that so God? His amazing character is to challenge us to do something He knows we aren't great at. And mine is asking for help.

Therapy wasn't a bad word in my home. My family supported the ongoing need to have someone to share your hardest and most secretive challenges with, and many times a therapist is just what the doctor orders. In the thick of my parents' cooperative divorce, my mom found an amazing therapist who helped me navigate my new life shift. When work stress became too much, I found a therapist who helped uncover more about my life, extending grace much further than any work worry. The pressures of a career, motherhood and more were caving in on me, and the foundational work she and I did together before I was impacted by a large corporate layoff was game-changing, life-changing even.

But something about my previous therapy experiences left me feeling still a bit cracked. I had found super glue to temporarily hold together my broken pieces, but whole never felt possible for me. The next shoe always lingered; I awaited its drop despite my positive attitude and optimistic nature, which continues to be a source of strength for me. But some weight is too hard for tiny cracks; super glue just won't suffice. This time, as I sat in the corner of my closet, I felt like the walls were inching closer. This time I knew I needed help and more than I had ever before.

Finding a therapist is like a treasure hunt for a new pair of shoes. It requires trial and error until you find the perfect fit, and believe me, the fit is more important than anything else. You need someone who understands you and is willing to listen to all you share through nonjudgmental eyes but is up for sharpening you in the process. You need a therapist who doesn't want you to wallow in your woes; you need one who teaches you where to find rope, how to weave it into a ladder and learn coping skills to pull yourself out of the pit.

A year prior, after receiving a chronic illness diagnosis, I had attempted to find a therapist for this phase of my life but to no avail. I planned to throw in the towel, but a friend recommended I give it another go. This time I knew what I was looking for in a therapist and used a website filter to find exactly who I needed. After God's prodding once more, I gave it a shot and added a new filter to my search: Christian therapy. Something I didn't even know existed, but I so desperately needed.

My faith had become my stronghold. It was the foundation for my steps and the lens through which I looked at life now.

Realizing I could find a therapist who spoke biblical truth offered new excitement for me. My filtered search highlighted only two in my area, but the moment I got off the phone with Rebekah, I knew she was the one to guide me through this dark moment.

What I didn't have clarity on just yet was that my soul needed to set my eyes on God's truths, at this moment and a future moment on the horizon. I had been trying to find my own rope to handcraft my own ladder when I really just needed to grab the rope God had stretched out to me all along.

Like a car, I expected I just needed a tune-up. A few visits would give me the boost necessary to get life back on track, I thought. I had a plan, but God giggled. He knew what was to come, and He knew I needed much more than an oil change. I needed an order change. Praise God for the foresight He has and for the persistence I have. I didn't know what was going to come, but He did, and He brought Rebekah into my life at the precise time to help me navigate it.

Months prior, Rebekah had listened to my worries. She had helped me create coping skills and strategies to tackle the consistent struggles I was facing. Through her guidance, she positioned me for forward momentum. But it was through her confidence in God that she taught me who was driving the car in the first place. I was doing a cruddy job of staying on the road; but when I gave the wheel over, I realized that God's got this. Different from every other therapist I'd worked with, Rebekah's insights were rooted in wisdom from God's truths. God is the healer. End of story. Stop looking for healing elsewhere; surrender it to Him. Not only can He carry the weight, but He can make good out of anything. He is the God who creates order from chaos, right!?

Her approach had already been life-changing, but it gave this momma a new form of surrendered ability on a day when I felt there was no hope left. I was able to do what the Shunammite woman did on the day when she could have felt like a puddle on the floor, and by today's standards, those feelings would have been warranted.

Instead, her response was one of surrender. *All is well.* And even when it doesn't feel that way, it really, truly is.

MAKE ROOM FOR GOD

Ever heard of the Shunammite woman? I'll be honest, I hadn't and many Christians I have chatted with haven't either! And yet, this woman who isn't called by her given name in Scripture has one of the most profound stories of faith, resilience and conviction I've ever studied. She is a woman we can all aspire to be, but it is her story of motherhood that inspires me most.

In 2 Kings 4:8, we first hear of her when Elisha was traveling to Shunem. Shunem[1] was a small village in the territory of Issachar and was noted as a landscape two times in core Scripture stories. It was where the Philistines camped before they battled Saul's army, and it was the setting of the miracle that happened with the Shunammite woman and her son. In Greek[2], Shunem means double resting place, and while it could pertain to the two story mentions, I am drawn to the two forms of resting that happen in the story of the Shunammite woman.

Elisha was a protégé of the prophet Elijah. Elijah trained him so he could continue to do God's powerful work after God took Elijah to heaven in a whirlwind (2 Kings 2:11). In fact, prior to his last day, Elijah asked Elisha a powerful question.

> "Tell me, what can I do for you before I am taken from
> you?" "Let me inherit a double portion of your spirit,"
> Elisha replied. "You have asked a difficult thing," Elijah said,
> "yet if you see me when I am taken from you, it will be yours
> —otherwise, it will not."
> 2 Kings 2:8-10 (NIV)

Elijah was an amazing prophet; Elisha received double the blessing. Imagine the impact his work would have with double the blessing and double the power.

So, as you can imagine, Elisha was busy. He was traveling a lot. And during his travels, he found himself from time to time in the town of

Shunem. From 2 Kings 4:8-10, we get a glimpse into the life-changing encounter that sets the stage for this beautiful story.

> One day Elisha went to Shunem. And a well-to-do woman
> was there, who urged him to stay for a meal. So whenever he
> came by, he stopped there to eat. She said to her husband, "I
> know that this man who often comes our way is a holy man
> of God. Let's make a small room on the roof and put in it a
> bed and a table, a chair and a lamp for him. Then he can
> stay there whenever he comes to us."
> 2 Kings 4:8-10 (NIV)

Here's what we know. The Shunammite woman was wealthy. Other translations refer to her as a leading, prominent, great woman. She was likely a woman with a bit of influence and clout in her community. Maybe she was a part of the town's welcoming committee, having a welcome basket prepared or the scent of freshly baked muffins permeating the air to draw people in. Possibly she had a little bakery in front of her home. I'm pretty confident that acts of service were her love language, and the conduit to make that happen was through full bellies. No ifs, ands or buts.

I smile reflecting on how both of my grandmas had this same desire. If you left their homes hungry, shame on you. They would whip something out of nothing to ensure that you left satisfied. You could taste the love my Grandma Lamaster put into her fried chicken and banana croquettes. And my Grandma Schrenger's Thanksgiving dressing was filled to the brim with love too. The Shunammite woman was likely known for her food as well. And, I bet Elisha came to love his trips through her town; he knew it was a place where he would be welcomed, and he would be fed. She had the means; Elisha had the growling belly.

We don't know how many times he had visited her before this encounter in Scripture, but I suspect it was plenty. It was enough for them to get past pleasantries and into deeper discussions. Ever want to know what's on someone's heart? Put them in front of a delicious hash-brown casserole, give them a slice or two of Derby pie or offer them a healthy scoop of spaghetti with my husband's homemade alfredo sauce, and they will tell all. I know I do! Food is good for the soul and a door opener to the heart's desires. If I were a betting woman, I'd bet the Shunammite woman, her husband and Elisha had many meals together before the instance that pushed her to take greater action, many opportunities to see he was a man who walked the walk and talked the talk. He was a man of God.

What does a man of God look like? Would I know one when I met him? Great question! Isn't the goal of God's people to be people who, when we walk by another, display crystal-clear evidence we are people of God? For me, I see God in people through their actions, how they treat people, what they talk about and what they don't. I see God in others by seeing how they see the world and how they treat others in it.

The Shunammite woman saw a holy man of God. She noticed his ways. And she said to her husband, "Hey, hon, I've been thinking. Let's create a room for Elisha so he can stay here on his travels. Whatcha say?" Can you imagine creating a room for a constant traveler who always stops by to eat when he's in town? (Wait… Is that what I'll experience when my kids are grown and flown?) Without hesitation, they create a room for him on their roof and fill it with a bed, table, chair and lamp. And, from that point forward, he would always have a place.

While Scripture highlights this as a physical room for a physical person, I can't help but consider what a pastor from Destination Church[3] suggested in a sermon on this topic. The Shunammite woman had discernment and listened to God's calling for her.

She wanted more of what Elisha had; she wanted a holy man of God to visit her home because she wanted God in her home. She made room for him and room for God. And, in doing so, she became blessed.

Elisha didn't overlook her kindness, just like God doesn't overlook ours. In 2 Kings 4:11-17, we learn of a beautiful blessing that Elisha gifts to her in exchange for the no-strings-attached kindness she had given him already.

> One day when Elisha came, he went up to his room and lay down there. He said to his servant Gehazi, "Call the Shunammite." So he called her, and she stood before him. Elisha said to him, "Tell her, 'You have gone to all this trouble for us. Now what can be done for you? Can we speak on your behalf to the king or the commander of the army?'" She replied, "I have a home among my own people." "What can be done for her?" Elisha asked. Gehazi said, "She has no son, and her husband is old." Then Elisha said, "Call her." So he called her, and she stood in the doorway. "About this time next year," Elisha said, "you will hold a son in your arms." "No, my lord!" she objected. "Please, man of God, don't mislead your servant!" But the woman became pregnant, and the next year about that same time she gave birth to a son, just as Elisha had told her.
> 2 Kings 4:11-17 (NIV)

We aren't told of what she held deep in her heart, but the Lord saw, and the Lord delivered because she made room for Him. As I turned to my therapist, Rebekah, for guidance, she kept pointing me to the One who heals. Had I made room for Him yet? Had I whispered into His ear my hardships?

Much like the Shunammite woman, I knew that I needed more God in my home, so, in the same place where I had dug my hole of despair, I began to see the place and space differently. Nothing good happens in the dark, I would tell myself. And yet, I began to see birth coming from a place of pitch-black hardship.

I bought some corkboard and pushpins. I rolled out my mat and turned on a dim lamp. I opened my Bible and turned my pit into a war room instead. And there, where I had felt that God was so distant once before, I began to make a room that was sacred and special for Him and me to convene.

Every morning, I began visiting this space. On my corkboard, I began pinning prayers, reminders and intentional requests next to the mini Polaroid photos my children took of themselves and most of our zoo of pets. Before the sun awoke, I would shake off sleep and meander to my special room where God and I would talk as I stretched the body He gave me, strengthening my muscles and building the stillness muscle that was very weak. Day after day, our relationship deepened. Day after day, as God and I moved past our pleasantries, I began to offer up deeper worries and concerns. And, day after day, God reminded me that He could carry it all.

As I was working through my internal struggles, the rest of my family was navigating their own as well. Preteen hormones were beginning to pop up like spring daffodils (although not as graceful and absolutely not as pretty). Sibling quarrels, friendship woes and boundary testing were leaving all of us exhausted, especially this momma.

Usually, I have thick skin and an ability to know what is worthy of worry and what I should let roll off my shoulders. But one particular day, I was caught off guard. My stomach leaped into my throat. The heat from blood rushing in my veins took over my face. And I was immobilized. Those feelings I had been keeping at bay decided it was time for an encore. But this time, I was ready.

My oldest had been my guinea pig for parenting, and let me just confirm what I am sure you know all too well: Raising children is anything but easy. This momma who can't stand injustice and loves deeply all people has a really, *really* hard time watching her kids navigate hardships where she feels like intervening may help. That evening, as I sat with my son on the oversized beanbag that I had purchased for our family to enjoy for movie nights, I realized I had no answers for his worries. I had no miracle salve that could fix what felt unfixable. A boo-boo kiss wouldn't do the trick. All I had was a listening ear and an aching momma heart. I felt lost.

He was navigating challenges anyone who lives in today's society will experience. The person he saw when he looked in the mirror and the person I saw when I looked at him appeared to not be the same. I saw a beautiful, beautiful boy with brown eyes that you could fall into. I daydreamed about his eyelashes, ones every girl swoons over and secretly wishes they had. You know the ones that look like they have mascara on without a mascara wand ever touching them. The freckles over his nose and cheeks looked like stars in a clear midnight sky, dreamy and twinkly. His heart was his best feature in my opinion, and how he saw the world was remarkable.

But that evening he sat on the beanbag and shared with me the struggles he was facing about how he saw himself, which was the polar opposite of how I did. Feelings of inadequacy had crept in. Our broken world was breaking him and me in the process. I spoke all the truths I knew of him and knew God had for him, but words fell short. He had made up his mind, and he had begun to believe the lies. I was heartbroken, sick even. I became worried and unsure of my next move. I didn't have a clue what to do beyond listening and praying, so that is what I did.

Later that evening, however, he had a mouthy preteen moment, and my parenting requirements came to a crossroads. One part of me wanted to hold him close and whisper sweet truths in his ears until I convinced his mind they were indeed facts. If he couldn't sway them, I was confident I could. The other part of me knew he needed to be disciplined for his poor behavior, and he required some alone time to reflect on his actions. He needed to go to bed early. I was fearful, though, of what alone time could do to my fragile baby. But it was the side of me that won the parenting fight.

To his room he went, and promptly to mine I went as well.
God was calling me.

REST IN HIM AND LEAVE THE REST TO HIM

"Don't blink." Sound advice parents like to impart to those new to the parenting club. Time, they say, goes by way too quickly. "The years are long, but the days are short" is a cliche I've heard on repeat, rolling my eyes at it until I finally understood. The parents before me were right. Each day feels like an eternity. But the weeks, months and years feel like light speed. The slow-down/speed-up conundrum follows parents everywhere they go. And, before they know it—in the blink of an eye—their kids grow up.

While unsure of the age of the Shunammite woman's son in 2 Kings 4:18-20, several pastors in my research suspected he was ten, maybe twelve when his life took a major shift.

> The child grew, and one day he went out to his father, who was with the reapers. He said to his father, "My head! My head!" His father told a servant, "Carry him to his mother." After the servant had lifted him up and carried him to his mother, the boy sat on her lap until noon, and then he died. 2 Kings 4:18-20 (NIV)

My heart. It stops when I read of instances where mothers lose their children. The order isn't right; it's out of order actually. Children aren't supposed to die first. It's just not supposed to happen that way. The Shunammite woman had received a blessing that she didn't even ask for directly but one her heart likely begged to experience. God gifted her a son, and for many years, she experienced the snotty noses, childhood belly laughs and healing hugs that come with being a mother. She wiped his tears and likely wept with him. We know she fed this boy in ways all our bellies can only wish for! She raised him in a home that knew God; and even had built a room for His prophet.

In a blink, the boy had grown.
And, in a blink, her world came crashing.

That day, as likely many days before, her son and her husband went out to work the land, helping the harvesters, when her son's head began to throb. All was well until it wasn't. His head pounded, and he screamed for help. Like most fathers today, the Shunammite woman's husband directed his son to be carried back to her. There's nothing more healing than a mother's touch, right? The Shunammite woman would know what to do. And, she did.

She began by holding him on her lap. For likely hours. They probably went out to harvest early in the day, before the sun's heat overtook their energy. And Scripture notes that the Shunammite woman held her son until noon when he died. Imagine her sitting in a chair or on the floor, grasping for anything while holding her everything, and rocking back and forth, whispering truths in his ear. I suspect she may have spoken these phrases through a waterfall of tears. I know I would have.

God promised. He won't let us down.
Hold on, sweet boy. God's got this.
I love you. God does too.

She didn't go running to the medicine cabinet looking for an earthly concoction. She didn't direct her husband to run to the nearest drug store for headache remedies.

She didn't look for healing from any place; instead, she went to the Healer.

She went up and laid him on the bed of the man of God, then shut the door and went out.
2 Kings 4:21 (NIV)

After her son died, she didn't begin funeral arrangements. Instead, she carried him upstairs to the room she and her husband had built for Elisha and laid him on the bed that the prophet rested on regularly. She found the physical strength to carry her son and the emotional strength to allow him to rest there while she went to the one who delivered the message of his birth and promised to not deceive her.

> She called her husband and said, "Please send me one of the servants and a donkey so I can go to the man of God quickly and return." "Why go to him today?" he asked. "It's not the New Moon or the Sabbath." "That's all right," she said. She saddled the donkey and said to her servant, "Lead on; don't slow down for me unless I tell you." So she set out and came to the man of God at Mount Carmel.
> 2 Kings 4:22-25 (NIV)

I imagine the Shunammite woman being one of the most poised and well-composed women to walk this earth. Her son had just died... in *her* arms. She carried his lifeless body up a flight of rickety stairs. She was breathless from the journey while her son was breathless from another. And as she closed the door, processing what had just happened and what she should do next, she called out to her husband with directives on what she needed his help with.

She didn't ask him to cry with her. She didn't command him to call the mortician. Instead, she asked for a servant and a donkey. She needed a driver and a vehicle; she was a momma on a mission and needed her getaway car. And pronto. Instead of trusting her, the woman who just laid her son to rest in the bed they created for the prophet, her husband had questions. He needed some details before he felt like he could take action.

I would have expected him to ask about their son's health. From what we are told in Scripture, we aren't even sure if the husband knows that the son didn't survive the unexpected aches and pains from earlier in the day. Instead, he questions why she needs to visit Elisha. In those times, the New Moon (or the first day of a new month) and the Sabbath were holy. Her husband was confused as to why she was visiting a holy man on just any ole day, not a holiday or a holy day. I'm suspecting he wasn't aware that it wasn't just any ole day; it was *the* day that would change their family's life.

Her response to her husband's confusion? Here are several translations to 2 Kings 4:23:

"That's all right," she said. (NIV)
"Don't let that bother you," she said. (NIRV)
But she said, "It will be all right." (NLT)
She said, "Don't ask questions; I need to go right now. Trust me." (MSG)
And she said, It shall be well. (KJV)

This isn't the first time she said "all would be well" when obviously it wasn't. And, it wouldn't be her last. She packed her bag, got on her donkey and went to find the man who promised to not deceive her, the man of God.

> When he saw her in the distance, the man of God said to his servant Gehazi, "Look! There's the Shunammite! Run to meet her and ask her, 'Are you all right? Is your husband all right? Is your child all right?'"
>
> "Everything is all right," she said.
>
> When she reached the man of God at the mountain, she took hold of his feet. Gehazi came over to push her away, but the man of God said, "Leave her alone! She is in bitter distress, but the Lord has hidden it from me and has not told me why."
>
> "Did I ask you for a son, my lord?" she said. "Didn't I tell you, 'Don't raise my hopes'?"
>
> Elisha said to Gehazi, "Tuck your cloak into your belt, take my staff in your hand and run. Don't greet anyone you meet, and if anyone greets you, do not answer. Lay my staff on the boy's face."

But the child's mother said, "As surely as the Lord lives and as you live, I will not leave you." So he got up and followed her.

Gehazi went on ahead and laid the staff on the boy's face, but there was no sound or response. So Gehazi went back to meet Elisha and told him, "The boy has not awakened."

When Elisha reached the house, there was the boy lying dead on his couch. He went in, shut the door on the two of them and prayed to the Lord. Then he got on the bed and lay on the boy, mouth to mouth, eyes to eyes, hands to hands. As he stretched himself out on him, the boy's body grew warm. Elisha turned away and walked back and forth in the room and then got on the bed and stretched out on him once more. The boy sneezed seven times and opened his eyes.

Elisha summoned Gehazi and said, "Call the Shunammite." And he did. When she came, he said, "Take your son." She came in, fell at his feet and bowed to the ground. Then she took her son and went out.
2 Kings 4:25-36 (NIV)

This time, the Shunammite woman traveled to Elisha and not the other way around. She had time to think during this trek; time to worry. But when Elisha saw her in the distance and sent Gehazi out to see what was the matter, her answer was the same as what she told her husband. With unwavering faith amidst her distress, she stated: "Everything is all right." Even when it wasn't, she knew it would be.

Elisha offered to send Gehazi and his staff to her son to see what he could do, but like the momma bear I suspect she was, she wasn't having it. Good try, old friend, but this momma isn't leaving without you, Elisha. Gehazi went and attempted to heal her son, but to no avail. The Shunammite woman knew Elisha was what she needed, not his staff. So, after likely several hours of time passing, Elisha reached the house and found her son dead on the bed.

Oh, to be a fly on the wall for the next scene in the Shunammite woman's story. Elisha lays on her dead son, his hands touching the boy's hands... his eyes touching the boy's eyes... his mouth breathing air into the boy's. Elisha laid face to face with death, looking it straight in the eyes and commanding it to leave. He felt the boy's body warm but yet, he grew defeated. He got up, walked back and forth, pacing the room and decided to not give up. He had work to do and his work wasn't finished. Again, he stretched out over him once more.

His hands held the boy's hands, guiding him back to life.
His eyes looked into the boy's eyes, seeing him with new life.
His mouth breathed air into the boy's mouth, calling him back to his mother.

The boy sneezed seven times and opened his eyes. He was resurrected! He sneezed out death and breathed in new life, a life that he was brought back to.

The Shunammite woman was right. All was well. God had this. God wasn't going to take away a blessing He had given her. Even in the hardest of moments, she knew what so few of us do. God is the giver of life; if He promised it, He won't let us down. Instead, we are called to rest in Him.

> Come to me, all you who are weary and burdened, and I will give you rest. Take my yoke upon you and learn from me, for I am gentle and humble in heart, and you will find rest for your souls. For my yoke is easy and my burden is light.
> Matthew 11:28-30 (NIV)

My own son laid on his bed, frustrated by my requirement of his early bedtime and challenged by the worries of his heavy heart. For the first time in my parenting journey and in a moment of helplessness, I chose a new path. I meandered to my war room nestled in my closet on the other side of the house. I rolled out my mat, turned on my lamp, opened my Bible and sat on the hardwood floor in tears. "God," I prayed. "I can't help him. Only you can. Please hold him close at this moment."

At that moment, while my son rested in his bed, I rested in my God, the One who heals. The One who doesn't break promises. The One who loves. The One who sees all. The One who resurrects. The One who can carry all worries. It was at that moment I felt an inner peace.

All would be well because He doesn't just want us to rest in Him, He wants us to leave the rest to Him.

NEW STORY FOR HIS GLORY

She came in, fell at his feet and bowed to the ground. Then she took her son and went out.
2 Kings 4:37 (NIV)

And there it was. The healing happened. She took her son and went out. That was that. Her life continued; her son's as well. The rest is history. Or, as Steven Furtick[4], pastor of Elevation Church, shared in one of his sermons on this topic, the rest is HIS story.

Immediately after we read in 2 Kings 4 of the Shunammite woman's son coming back to life, we learn of a new hardship she and her family are soon to face. In 2 Kings 4:38, we are told: "Elisha returned to Gilgal and there was a famine in the region." As if the struggles she just endured weren't enough, now her family is forced to deal with another.

There is no time for celebrating. Instead, Elisha tells the Shunammite woman:

"Go away with your family and stay for a while wherever you can, because the Lord has decreed a famine in the land that will last seven years." The woman proceeded to do as the man of God said. She and her family went away and stayed in the land of the Philistines seven years.
2 Kings 8:1-2 (NIV)

And, because she's a woman of faith who just witnessed a miracle, she does what she always has; she trusts, and she follows.

We aren't told of what her and her son's lives were like in those seven years, but I can only imagine. She likely found herself staring into her son's eyes, grateful to see life in them again. She probably wept in the quiet nights, shedding tears of joy and gratitude as she deepened her relationship with God. I'm sure she had a new pep to her step and a lightness in her heart despite the famine around her because she was proven, yet again, that the God she loves sees her, hears her cries and cares deeply for her and her family. She had survived losing her son; surely she could survive the famine.

At the end of the seven years, we are told in 2 Kings 8 that the Shunammite woman returned to her land; she and her family were ready to go home. There was just one problem; her home had been taken, and she needed to go to the king to request it back. If I didn't know her character by now, I would say that could have become a stressful situation. But this is the woman who is calm, cool and collected. I can imagine she told her husband and son that all would be well. And, to no surprise, it was.

> At the end of the seven years she came back from the land of the Philistines and went to appeal to the king for her house and land. The king was talking to Gehazi, the servant of the man of God, and had said, "Tell me about all the great things Elisha has done." Just as Gehazi was telling the king how Elisha had restored the dead to life, the woman whose son Elisha had brought back to life came to appeal to the king for her house and land.

Gehazi said, "This is the woman, my lord the king, and this is her son whom Elisha restored to life." The king asked the woman about it, and she told him.

Then he assigned an official to her case and said to him, "Give back everything that belonged to her, including all the income from her land from the day she left the country until now."
2 Kings 8:3-6 (NIV)

Steven Furtick's sermons on the Shunammite woman challenged me to see her story through a new lens; her story was a part of His story and became a part of history through a series of "God-sequences." Let's look at the play-by-play.

- Because the Shunammite woman loved to care for travelers, feed the community and was a part of the welcoming committee, she had the opportunity to notice Elisha and welcomed him in for a meal or two or twenty.
- Because she spent time getting to know him, she could tell he was a man of God and wanted a bit more of that in her home. She told her husband of her desire to make a room for Elisha, and he obliged.
- Because Elisha traveled often and the Shunammite woman noticed he needed a room, she built him one and furnished it. That room was his resting place and became the near-final resting place of her son when he died unexpectedly. But she didn't give up on her son or her God.
- Because Elisha had learned from Elijah, he was doubly ready to do double the blessings and after double the trying was able to bring the Shunammite woman's son back from the dead.
- Because the Shunammite woman trusted Elisha when he told her to leave for seven years because of the famine, she returned at just the right moment when Gehazi was telling

the king about the miracles Elisha had done and her family's miracle story.

- Because she was walking proof of what Elisha (and God) could do, the Shunammite woman and her family didn't just get their home back, the king also gave her all the income from the land from the day she left the country up until that point. She got what she wanted and more!

God knew the trajectory of her story, but it all started when she decided to create a room in her home, and subsequently a new story to her life. What was likely the worst day of her life became her best and served as an opportunity to see, yet again, how God was and is working in her everything.

As I consider the Shunammite woman's new story, I'm reminded of how God has made a new story in my life too. Here's my play-by-play.

- Because of my past hardships, I was keenly aware of when I needed help again. My family's openness to therapy created an openness in my heart to find someone to help me with new struggles.
- Because I believe nothing good happens in the dark, I spoke with a friend regarding my bout of situational depression, and she encouraged me to find a therapist through a new tool, opening my eyes to Christian therapy, not something I had ever known of.
- Because I had spent time with my therapist months prior to that hard day with my son, I already had the coping skills in place and knew where to turn to and who to turn to when I felt all hope was gone. I knew God could handle it when I couldn't.
- Because I had created a room for Him in my home, physically, my family began to see how God was all around us and within us. My daughter even mentioned one day when my husband and I pass away and she has the house (her dream, I guess) that she would use the war room for

her prayer time. "Sweet girl," I told her. "Don't wait until then. Come pray with me now."

- Because of my relationship with God, I was able to surrender my parenting hardship to Him (and continue to do so to this day). I still stumble and fall, but God is always catching me. And, He caught my son that day too; the next morning, all was well.
- Because of each step, my faith is strengthened. The way I parent now has changed some and I am getting better, day by day, at letting God lead me instead of me thinking I can take the reins.

When we bring God into our homes, into our thoughts, into our parenting approach, into our work, into our relationships, into everything—everything changes. We create a new story, not just for us but for those around us and our children, too. And, this new story isn't for our glory. Friends, it's for His.

THE WOMAN WITH NO NAME WAS A MOTHER OF MANY WORDS

A powerhouse of her era, the mother bear of all momma bears, the Shunammite woman may not be known by her name in Scripture, but she is known by her words and actions.

"Don't mislead your servant!"

2 Kings 4:16 can be translated in many ways. She begged Elisha to not lie to her, asking him to not play games or tease her with fantasies. She prayed to not be deceived or misled by Elisha's words that a year later she would have a son. She didn't want him to get her hopes up.

Ever felt like that in your prayerful life? Ever begged God to not promise you something that you deeply desire only to have it ripped from your grasp? That was the heart of her statement here. She likely always wanted a child but was struggling to make that a reality. She didn't want to get a bite of opportunity to not have the pleasure of enjoying its entirety.

I suspect that after she said this to Elisha and then, a year later, held her beautiful baby boy, she had a peace knowing that what God promises, He delivers. He gave her this boy; surely He wouldn't take him away. The contentment she had even as despair gripped her heart on her darkest of days had to come from this moment where she told the man of God that she didn't want to taste motherhood without getting all of it. And she was trusting that God wouldn't steal it from her.

As my children grow, I am grateful for the reminder of how our God works. He doesn't mislead us or lie to us. He doesn't deceive us or play games with us. Our God loves us deeply and hears us. God brings life, always and in all ways.

"Everything is all right."

The Shunammite woman wasn't a "fake it till you make it" momma. She knew everything was all right. She knew it when she laid her son on Elisha's bed. She knew it when she reached Elisha and asked him to come to their home. And she knew it when she went to get her land and home back. From our perspective, everything was far from right, but from her perspective, she had faith that God makes things right.

Her trust wasn't in what she saw but in what she knew.

Do you have that level of faith?! (In a hushed whisper I'm pledging to you that I'm not fully there yet.) When the going gets hard, where do you take your worries? Can you be content through all situations, even the toughest of ones? Where do you take things in your life that feel dead or dying? All hard questions with a simple (but hard to fully believe) answer: God.

The only way through this parenting nonsense, Momma, is to turn to the only One who can handle the heaviness you carry, the worries that swarm you and the seemingly dead that you want to bring back to life. God's got this. He has water for the weary, fertilizer for new growth and peace that He offers in exchange for those worries. And when you begin to know all is well, your family will see, and your children will take notice. More than anything, your children will find solace in God when they see you turning to Him first.

She told him.

In 2 Kings 8:6, the king asks the Shunammite woman about the story Gehazi told him about Elisha restoring her son to life. He was curious about her side of the story because, as we know, there is always my side, your side and the truth. Was this man legit? The king wanted to know.

The Shunammite woman could have said nothing. She could have told a partial story. But that's not what is documented in Scripture. Instead, she told him. She shared her testimony. She told all. She didn't hold back details. She gave God the glory. And, she had walking proof; her son was standing next to her. Because she told her story, she was given even more.

Her parenting journey was all but easy. Every twist and turn showed up in her story. And, instead of living with lemons, she chose to consistently make sweet, sweet lemonade. She didn't worry about the past; God's got this. She didn't fret about the future; God's paving the way. Instead, she was content in all of it, telling her story which is now a part of yours.

Heavenly Father, help me rest in you and leave the rest to you. During hardships, times of worry and doubt, moments of fear and uncertainty, remind me that you're happy to carry all the burden and remind me to fully surrender my concerns to you. Thank you for your willingness to carry me and my worries always, no questions asked. Your love for me is enough. I pray that I can find the level of contentment you desire for my heart so that I can confidently say and believe that everything is all right. In Jesus's name, Amen.

6

ELIZABETH
THE MOTHER OF GRACE

Shannon Carroll

S o many crazy things happened in our life during the season when we lived on Hancock Road in Scottsburg, near our church. It was the epicenter of our amnesia journey. It's the seat of so many precious memories our kids have of their childhood, with chickens, garden life, Nerf gun fights and box forts in the backyard. I learned to can green beans, pick peaches and hatch chicks while we lived in this home. We started homeschooling there. I launched a wellness business and hosted countless beautiful people in that space. It's the street where I grew up as a woman in many ways.

And *she* lived across the street. One of the biggest blessings of our time in that home was our relationship with our precious neighbor. As a dear grandma herself, she took my boys under her wing. She instilled a love of cooking within Evan as she patiently taught him how to make delicious sausage balls and enchiladas. She gave him his first job of vacuuming, dusting, picking up sticks and taking care of their sweet dog. Evan was so proud of his first check, earning ten dollars an hour—he even got a dollar raise from her that first year because of his stellar work ethic! After getting his work done, he remembers sitting down to play Scrabble with her. Every moment was filled with so much love and intentional purpose.

Not only did our chickens like to migrate across the road to free range in her yard (we still never figured out why they crossed the road!), but I also found myself drawn down the path to her home. She took me in and mentored me in such an easy yet profound way. We'd sit and rock on her front porch while drinking tea, talking about life and then praying together. In the winter months, we moved into her warm and cozy kitchen, where we'd sit at the kitchen counter and talk about life, mothering, being a godly wife, and so on.

As a pastor's wife with so many demands on me from other women, it was extra special to have my person who poured back into me. I could cry, share deep parts of my hurting soul and read my journal to her. She'd listen and then respond with godly wisdom, much of which I recorded as she talked. Throughout the week, she'd pray for me and jot down nuggets and insights to share when we got together. I will forever treasure the time we lived across the street from each other.

My neighbor was my Elizabeth. As I studied this amazing mother in Scripture and tried to picture what she looked like, all I could think about was my sweet neighbor. To me, she was a godly mentor, a spirit-filled mother, a loving grandmother with arms long enough to stretch around my boys. She exuded wisdom and grace in every way and in every encounter. She loved the Lord and spoke of her relationship with Him with such passion and intimacy. Being around her, I wanted to love Jesus (as well as my husband and kids) like she did. What a gift.

If you've had an Elizabeth in your life, you know exactly what I'm talking about. Maybe you are an Elizabeth to someone else!

Elizabeth, as we will see in our deep-dive study of her life, was a rare gem of a wife and mother. She had the purest of hearts toward the Lord. She loved her husband, even through his obvious faults. She quietly bore the pain of barrenness and loneliness. She embraced her role as mentor to the mother of Jesus, and in crucial times when the world was watching, she responded to conflict and difficulty with grace and truth.

When I think of a Spirit-filled mother, I think of Elizabeth. She is the type of woman most Christian women want to be like—or at least we should want to emulate her. Centuries later, her life calls to us as an example and a challenge.

WHAT SCRIPTURE TELLS US ABOUT ELIZABETH

Elizabeth is only mentioned in a section of one chapter in all of Scripture, yet what we glean from these verses is quite moving. She is introduced to us as living in the days of Herod (Luke 1:5). From history, we know these were terrible days of persecution for the Jews with the Roman occupation. The Jews were clinging to the Old Testament prophecies of a coming Messiah to rescue them from tyranny and ungodly rulers. Life at this time was not easy.

We see early on in our story that Elizabeth is married to Zacharias, a Levite priest. Elizabeth herself is of Levite descent, and both of them are described as: "Righteous in the sight of God, walking blamelessly in all the commandments and requirements of the Lord" (Luke 1:6, NASB).

This is quite a character commendation. Zacharias and Elizabeth came from top-notch Jewish stock, and they were quite the high-performing, godly religious couple. They took their religion very seriously as they studied the Torah and sought to obey it to the best of their abilities. This summation of their life does not mean that they were perfect, but their hearts were turned toward the Lord, and they lived a beautiful testimony of Him before others.

But before we start to think that they were so good that they had no trouble in their lives, the very next verse gives us a clue about one of their deep, intimate, painful struggles.

> But they had no child, because Elizabeth was barren, and they were both advanced in years.
> Luke 1:7 (NASB)

None of us, no matter our impeccable upbringing or devotion to the Lord, are immune to difficulty and suffering. It's a part of our very existence on this fallen planet. We don't know how old Elizabeth was at this time, but she was quite obviously past her prime for childbearing. It appeared that the door of opportunity had closed for her, and this had caused Elizabeth and Zacharias great pain and anguish. The capability to have children was seen as a significant blessing, especially in that culture. A woman's worth was often found in her ability to have children and continue a family line. Not being able to get pregnant or maintain a pregnancy was a source of shame in those days. Her heart was broken, and she carried a wound from this stigma.

What I love about this story is that there's no indication that they ever became bitter toward the Lord during their grief and sadness. They continued being blameless before Him, praying and serving Him in the temple and their lifestyle day after day. Their hearts remained tender toward the Lord—and it's the softened heart that the Lord loves to use and work through in HIMpossible ways.

I love the phrase in verse eight, "Now it happened." My friend, we know that nothing happens by accident. God wasn't surprised by what took place next in the story. No, in fact, He orchestrated it all!

One day Zacharias is chosen to go into the Holy of Holies for an annual ritual; this is a once-in-a-lifetime priestly duty. There are high standards for the priest to enter the inner sanctuary to burn incense on behalf of the people. It was the pinnacle of Zacharias's career! As he stood near the altar of incense, an angel suddenly appeared to him. As you and I would also probably be, Zacharias was startled and afraid.

The angel proclaimed some outlandish and incredible declarations to Zacharias in this next section of Scripture (Luke 1:13-17).

- God has heard their prayers!
- They will bear a son.
- His name needs to be John.
- Zacharias and Elizabeth will have joy and gladness.
- Many will rejoice at his birth.
- John will be great in the sight of the Lord.
- He will be set apart and should not drink wine.
- He will be filled with the Holy Spirit *while in his mother's womb*.
- He will be instrumental by the Lord in turning many of the Israelites back to the Lord.
- He will be called as a forerunner for the Messiah.
- His ministry will be in the spirit of Elijah, turning the hearts of the fathers back to the children and to make ready a people prepared for the Lord.

Imagine if an angel suddenly appeared and told you all of these things about your future child. You and I would probably struggle to comprehend and absorb all of this. I wouldn't be surprised if Zacharias got stuck just after the very first line item delivered by the angel—that they were finally going to have a child! And this wouldn't be just any ordinary child. Their son would be part of God's prophetic, universal, eternal, redemptive plan. This would be a glorious—but hard—pill for any of us to swallow, especially in that moment. Yet when the Lord speaks, we are to listen and believe wholeheartedly in faith.

Zacharias, like you and me, needed to confirm and clarify what he had just heard. With some doubt in his heart, he dared to ask a question of this angelic messenger: "How will I know this for

certain? For I am an old man and my wife is advanced in years"
(Luke 1:18, NASB).

These are legitimate questions. However—note to self—if the angel
Gabriel ever shows up to you or to me and gives a powerful, hard-
to-believe message, our immediate response needs to be, "Yes, sir!"
God is looking for hearts completely sold out to Him and willing to
do and believe whatever He says. Zacharias will pay a steep consequence for entertaining doubtful thoughts.

> The angel answered and said to him, "I am Gabriel, who
> stands in the presence of God, and I have been sent to speak
> to you and to bring you this good news. And behold, you
> shall be silent and unable to speak until the day when these
> things take place, because you did not believe my words,
> which will be fulfilled in their proper time."
> Luke 1:19-20 (NASB)

Yikes! That's a pretty severe punishment. I'm taking parenting notes
from how God taught Zacharias this lesson; he made the punishment fit the crime for sure, and the consequence was quite thorough
and pretty tough. God is serious about us believing Him and His
Word in faith.

Zacharias would have ten long months to play this encounter over
and over again in his mind. This time of silence would change his
heart forever and cause him to deepen his trust in the Lord. Even
those of us who have been believers for a long time sometimes have
to learn lessons the hard way.

God has a pattern of taking away some of our senses in an effort to
get our attention and teach us lessons. He took away the eyesight
from Christian-hater Saul as he was transforming into the apostle
Paul. He removed Zacharias's ability to speak for several months as
He did some heart surgery on him. In my personal life, I can testify
that God scooped out my husband's memories for twenty-six days as
a way to get our attention and show us that we needed to make
some major changes in how we were living. Nothing is out of the

reach of God's scalpel if He believes it will be for our good and His glory.

I wonder what life was like in the home with Zacharias and Elizabeth as he had to silently scribble out his encounter with the angelic messenger and communicate with his wife. I'm sure he was humble and tender, as we all should be after receiving discipline from the Lord. Amid Elizabeth's joy for her promised son, she was also juggling a hurting husband.

I can relate to her feeling of being caught in the middle, wanting to protect him and communicate on his behalf while also dealing with her own emotions and needs. I felt this very deeply while my David suffered from amnesia. It's hard.

As the story goes, Elizabeth conceived—praise the Lord! She decided to hide herself for the first five months. I'm sure she had more than the usual early pregnancy emotions; there was a lot to process and ponder. It's hard to present a celebratory front when there are years of trauma and pain right under the surface. I wonder if she felt any shame for her husband's temporary mutism, which most likely had already been gossiped about throughout the entire town. It was a quiet period in Elizabeth's life—in more ways than one.

Near the middle of Elizabeth's pregnancy, the same angel appears to Mary to deliver the news that she will become the mother of Jesus, the Messiah. Mary conceives in Elizabeth's sixth month of pregnancy. Amid rumors and scandals and uncertainty, Mary leaves her home and quickly travels to Elizabeth. Some Bible versions say they are cousins; others translate the familial relationship as just relatives. Regardless, the angel thought it relevant to tell Mary about Elizabeth's miraculous conception—and it had the desired effect of Mary going to be with Elizabeth.

God is working overtime and in supernatural ways in both women's lives and pregnancies—Elizabeth is beyond childbearing years, and Mary has never been with a man. Yet both of them are promised to carry and deliver world-changers. I can't even begin to imagine what they were feeling and thinking. But thank the Lord that they had each other. I guarantee their relationship during those sweet three months they spent together provided invaluable support and encouragement for both of them on this unique and lonely journey.

I love this moment that is captured for all of history when Elizabeth first hears Mary's voice as she runs to greet her:

> When Elizabeth heard Mary's greeting, the baby leaped in her womb; and Elizabeth was filled with the Holy Spirit. And she cried out with a loud voice and said, "Blessed are you among women, and blessed is the fruit of your womb! And how has it happened to me, that the mother of my Lord would come to me? For behold, when the sound of your greeting reached my ears, the baby leaped in my womb for joy. And blessed is she who believed that there would be a fulfillment of what had been spoken to her by the Lord."
> Luke 1:41-45 (NASB)

There's so much to unpack here! But first, I want to know what that sensation was. Not only was she filled with the Holy Spirit, but her baby was as well. That had to be more than a normal kick and punch made from inside the womb. I'm sure it was an intense, overwhelming, warm, joy-filled feeling—unlike anything she had ever experienced in her life!

> The Holy Spirit was all over these women and their babies. He was inside of them, surrounding them and speaking through them. They had church right then and there.

We finish our retelling of Elizabeth's story when it's time for her to give birth. (Have you noticed all the references to time in this chapter? Truly, our times are in His hands. Psalm 31:15) Read the rest of this powerful story and see if you can picture it all playing out just as it's written.

Now the time had come for Elizabeth to give birth, and she gave birth to a son. Her neighbors and her relatives heard that the Lord had displayed His great mercy toward her; and they were rejoicing with her. And it happened that on the eighth day they came to circumcise the child, and they were going to call him Zacharias, after his father. But his mother answered and said, "No indeed; but he shall be called John." And they said to her, "There is no one among your relatives who is called by that name." And they made signs to his father, as to what he wanted him called. And he asked for a tablet and wrote as follows, "His name is John." And they were all astonished. And at once his mouth was opened and his tongue loosed, and he began to speak in praise of God... All who heard them kept them in mind saying, "What then will this child turn out to be?" For the hand of the Lord was certainly with him... And the child continued to grow and to become strong in spirit, and he lived in the deserts until the day of his public appearance to Israel.
Luke 1:57-64, 66, 80 (NASB)

Wow! Zacharias and Elizabeth's quiet, simple life had been turned upside down by a visit from God. The world was watching their responses to all that was happening, and it caused them to wonder what was going on with this special child as well. God was stirring things up and getting everyone's attention. His hand was on this entire, precious family.

Names have special meanings in Scripture. Zacharias's name means, "remembered of Jehovah." God didn't forget Zacharias; He confirmed that He heard his prayers and remembered him for a very important assignment as the father of John the Baptist.

Elizabeth means "oath of God." Could it be that by putting Zacharias and Elizabeth together, God was sending a sign to the whole world that He had not forgotten His people, but He was actively fulfilling the prophecies and oaths promised for generations that a Messiah was coming to save His people? Their lives were a testament to the faithfulness of God.

ROLES AND RESPONSIBILITIES

As I was listening to various sermons and reading a few commentaries about the story of Elizabeth, someone mentioned that she was the first person in Scripture to call Jesus as Lord. What a high honor! This happened when Mary arrived in Elizabeth's home and Elizabeth exclaimed, "And how has it happened to me, that the mother of my Lord would come to me?" She recognized the divine hand all over this story, and she had faith to believe that the Messiah was inside the womb of her dear relative Mary.

Elizabeth can be seen as the glue in her family. Do you have anyone in your family that acts as the glue? My mother is the main hub of the wheel in our family and among her sisters. She has a definite ministry to the family, immediate and extended. It's where she thrives and shines as she serves, prays for, feeds and blesses everyone. When my mom was very sick last year, the whole family rallied to pray for and cheer her on to recovery; we can't imagine living life without my mom as the glue.

Elizabeth was this person. Zacharias needed her stabilizing and grounding influence in his suffering and discipline. They obviously had talked before John's birth, and Elizabeth was convinced of the report that Zacharias wrote out. She trusted him. She defended him in front of the crowd. She supported him, and she loved him through it all.

Mary also depended on Elizabeth's mentorship and unconditional love in the first trimester of her very unique and unplanned pregnancy. I wish all of their discussions within those three months were recorded for us. I believe Elizabeth helped give Mary confidence for the road ahead.

And finally, even though we don't have any records of how Elizabeth trained and reared her son, John, we know her life had a profound influence on him. God placed John the Baptist with his specific parents for a reason. I'm sure John loved his mother greatly.

I also like to think of Elizabeth as a pastor's wife. From the text, it sounds like Zacharias might have been gone overnight when it was his turn to rotate through the priestly duties at the temple. She had to share him with the high calling of serving God's people in His temple. She understood the need to make sacrifices. She felt the fishbowl effect of her position, knowing everyone was watching her life.

At times, she probably knew she needed to retreat for a season and let the world go on without her. Elizabeth had a front-row seat to watch her husband shine and struggle; she knew firsthand that he wasn't perfect. Yet she never wavered in her devotion to and support of him. I can relate to all of this, and I find comfort in Elizabeth's mature example of how she handled herself in her role as "wife of the priest."

BROKEN TO BEAUTIFUL

Even though Elizabeth had it going on in so many areas of her life —great upbringing, she loved the Lord, her husband had a stable and respectable position, she followed the commands completely with her whole heart and had a wonderful reputation—she, like us, experienced deep brokenness and wounds.

She was barren, a significant type of curse in her society. She keenly felt the reproach of her condition. I imagine she battled thoughts of unworthiness, not being enough, not being seen. Those who have battled infertility for years can relate to her inner thoughts and torments. It feels as if the world is moving on without you and that somehow you are second-hand goods. Our identity as women is so closely intertwined with our fertility. But this doesn't allow much room for living in a fallen world where our cycles don't always line up with our normal, natural goals and desires.

The battle is real for countless women. The broken pieces seem impossible to ever put back together.

I wonder if Elizabeth had given up on waiting each month for a sign of hope. Had she closed the door on that chapter and resigned herself to never having children?

We know that God had both her and Zacharias wait past the point of normal, much like He did for Abraham and Sarah. I'm noticing a pattern where God takes us beyond the point where we think we can handle it one more second, just a hair past that moment of desperation and surrender before He steps in with a miraculous intervention.

Elizabeth endured the brokenness of her husband and realized that the entire community possibly knew the reason for his forced silence was because he dared to "talk back" to the angelic messenger Gabriel. Sensing her husband's public shame had to have been a difficult cross to bear, all while sensing new life growing inside of her. The juxtaposition of emotions was severe.

Elizabeth knew brokenness like you and I understand it. And yet, like so many other women in Scripture, she also lived a powerful broken to beautiful story.

Her marriage stayed strong and I'm sure got even stronger as they presented a unified front before questioning neighbors and relatives. God turned her aging barrenness into a fruitful womb. Favor was restored to her. The Holy Spirit fell on and in her and on the child she carried within her. She gave birth to a child who had a strong spirit and purpose.

I love it when God writes the last chapter, and it's better than anyone could have ever imagined! Elizabeth cultivated the heart and attitude that allowed God to reach in and redeem every single broken piece. He is able to do the same for you and for me.

LESSONS WE CAN LEARN FROM ELIZABETH

We've already encountered several lessons we can learn from the one chapter that gives us a few special sneak peeks into the life and character of Elizabeth. I hope you're already growing to love this mature, Spirit-filled mother like I am. I want to reach my golden years and have her charm, grace and grit. Here are a few more lessons we can glean from her story.

God takes each of us on a waiting journey of sanctification.

I remember being in my early twenties and thinking I'd never find my husband. The waiting in those pre-marriage years is so incredibly hard. Whether it's waiting for God to reveal our future spouse or waiting to see the double pink line on the pregnancy test, waiting for a diagnosis, waiting for our children to hit the next stage so we can finally sleep at night, or waiting for the perfect opportunity to land the dream job, we are all most likely waiting on something.

Waiting feels painful and like it's never going to end while we're focused on the end goal. Yet waiting is actually a biblical season. The Psalms are full of verses all about waiting. If you are currently waiting for something, you're probably right where God wants you to be. He does some of His best work while we're waiting. Why is that?

While we're waiting, we typically talk to God a lot more than normal. We're asking Him what His will is, seeking and looking for it around every bend. We're thinking about Him and observing how He's orchestrating our life. Waiting requires the surrender of our timetable and expectations. God prunes us while we wait and allows the waiting to cause us to depend on Him even more, which is His ultimate goal for our sanctification.

> Wait for the Lord;
> Be strong and let your heart take courage;
> Yes, wait for the Lord.
> Psalm 27:14 (NASB)

Elizabeth waited a long time for her answer. I believe the waiting created a gentle, grateful spirit in her. If we got everything we wanted when we wanted it, we'd all be spoiled brat Christians. The next time you find yourself in a season of waiting, thank God for it. Immerse yourself in the Psalms and build your faith muscle, as you eagerly anticipate and watch for His hand to move in your life.

Sanctification is taking place while you wait.

God has blessings and spiritual fruit for us even in advanced age.

I don't know why we think that we have to be in our prime of life to be useful and meaningful in God's kingdom. The way our world glorifies youth and disregards our elderly is quite shameful. Those who are a few years older than we are typically have so much wisdom and insight to share.

I love sitting with the matriarchs at our church and listening to them talk about their lives and their Lord. Women who have been married fifty-plus years give the greatest marriage advice!

Gray hair truly is a sign of wisdom. Elizabeth's life is a testament that God still has work for us to do even when we are "past the point" of whatever threshold we've created in our minds. My husband often says that retirement is not in the Bible—that we are never to press pause on our spiritual and evangelistic work and just coast our way through the pearly gates. There is work to be done by all of us in every season of life, including our latter half.

And even when I am old and gray, O God, do not
forsake me,
Until I declare Your strength to this generation and your
power to all who are to come.
Psalm 71:18 (NASB)

The enemy tries to tell us we're all dried up, no one wants to hear from us anymore; our aches and pains should prevent us from getting up to serve. There is a true battle against aging. Yet, God tells us that there is beauty in aging, and He can use us in every season of life, as long as we have breath.

If you're in the golden years of your life and you've struggled with feeling like you don't have a purpose, then I pray the story of Elizabeth has encouraged you. I pray you have a renewed vigor to seek out where God wants you to produce fruit. He has something for you! It might be as the prayer warrior and intercessor for your kids, grandchildren and inner circle. It might be as a mentor to younger women, discipling them in the ways of the Lord. Your calling might be to teach or sing or visit or write cards. I don't know specifically what God is speaking to your heart—but I know if you listen, He will direct you.

And if you are in the younger generation, please let's be more intentional about honoring and seeking out the wisdom of those who have gone before us. Pray that God will send you an Elizabeth to help mentor and guide you along life's path. It should be a goal of every church to pair each younger lady with an older lady as part of their discipleship program. I believe marriages would be changed if each new wife had an older woman to help guide her through the early years of marriage. Families would be eternally impacted by an older woman helping the younger women navigate child-raising and rearing.

Elizabeth was a beautiful, mature, older woman. I know she loved younger Mary in such a special and supportive way as Mary sought out the wisdom and encouragement of her older relative. God puts the right people in our lives at the right time. Young and old alike – and everyone in between—let's honor the grace and beauty that comes with aging and understand that until we take our dying breath, we have a purpose and we can bear fruit.

Great impact requires great sacrifice and suffering.

Elizabeth and Zacharias had to go through quite a bit of painful pruning since they were being commissioned as the parents of a child with the spirit of Elijah on him. I've learned in life that anyone who will make a great impact on the kingdom of God will encounter (extra?) trials and tribulations. Take a moment and look up one of your heroes of the faith—someone like Corrie Ten Boom, Elizabeth Elliot, and so on. As you read their stories, you'll learn that suffering was a significant part of their testimony.

> Consider it all joy, my brethren, when you encounter
> various trials, Knowing that the testing of your faith
> produces endurance. And let endurance have its perfect
> result, so that you may be perfect and complete, lacking in
> nothing.
> James 1:2-4 (NASB)

Pruning produces more fruit in the gardening world, and it does the exact same thing in our hearts. As more of the flesh is cut away and as we learn to lean more on the Lord and His Spirit, we have more room for Him to flow through us and use us. To look more like Him, we have to first have more of us removed from the picture. This process is painful and hard. We will shed tears. But the ultimate prize awaits and is before us!

The world is watching how we respond to tragedy and triumph.

There are several references in Elizabeth's story to the crowd. They were waiting outside when Zacharias encountered the angel. Elizabeth hid from them when she first learned she was pregnant. They were back again, watching and evaluating, when the new parents arrived to dedicate and name their child.

We learned very quickly during our amnesia season that the world was watching our story as we were living it. I've never had so many Facebook likes and comments as when I was posting daily updates about our real-time struggle. Maybe it's that we all love looking at a car wreck, or maybe it's that we are drawn to stories of tragedy and triumph.

Our human nature looks for the overcomer in the midst of a messy situation.

We have the opportunity as believers to live our lives out loud, to let the world watch us live and suffer and celebrate—and to point them to Christ in every interaction and instance. We don't have to be perfect, but we do need to be real. When we mess up, we need to own it. The world appreciates transparency and realness. Whether we are living our faith and life out loud on social media or around the water cooler at work, be aware that others are watching.

Unborn children are precious in God's sight.

Two of the major characters in this story are unborn babies. It's very clear from the story that God values the life of the unborn and considers them human even while in the womb. The account of John the Baptist leaping in the womb when he sensed the presence of the Messiah growing in Mary is absolutely mind-blowing. The Holy Spirit came upon and in an unborn baby—how miraculous is that?

> For You formed my inward parts;
> You wove me together in my mother's womb.
> I will give thanks to You, for I am fearfully and wonderfully made.
> Psalm 139:13-14 (NASB)

Just as these precious mothers honored, celebrated and respected their unborn children, so should we. This attitude is in direct contrast to the philosophy of the world. Even during Elizabeth's time, Herod was on a rampage to kill babies because of the threat of the soon-to-be-delivered Messiah, as revealed to him by the wise men. Evil rulers have always perpetuated the killing of innocent children and unborn babies.

Our own country is no different. In a recent State of the Union address, the current president angrily chanted about the "right" of women to kill their unborn children, to the cheers of the congressional mob. I'm afraid we will experience judgment for this as a nation.

Let's call back to the truth of God's Word and uphold what He says is sacred. He created all life, and all life is valuable in His sight. This story is a powerful confirmation of that eternal truth.

A word of grace to mothers who have walked through the valley of abortion. Please know that total forgiveness is extended to you if you ask for it. God can redeem your broken pieces and heal your past. This doesn't define you anymore if you are a daughter of the King.

SPIRIT-FILLED MOTHERHOOD

As I've spent hours studying the life of Elizabeth and wondering what aspect of motherhood she would teach us, I was consistently drawn to the number of times the text highlighted the Holy Spirit. It was prophesied that the Spirit would be upon John. We learn that the Holy Spirit fell on Elizabeth when she heard Mary's greeting, and the Spirit was on John the Baptist while he was still in her womb.

Zacharias was filled with the Spirit when he got his voice back, and he burst into praise and prophecy. This is extra remarkable because, at this time, the Spirit was not given to all the believers until Pentecost, after Jesus's death, resurrection and ascension. The Holy Spirit is a major theme of this section of Scripture. Let's take a look at what Elizabeth shows us Spirit-filled motherhood looks like.

A Spirit-filled mother is solid in her walk with God first.

Throughout these verses, we see that Zacharias and Elizabeth had fully given their hearts to the Lord. There are multiple prayers and conversations they had with the Lord just in this one chapter. When we are first introduced to them, we learn that they were blameless before the Lord. Their hearts were pure, and they were completely dedicated to Him. This is a sign of a Spirit-filled mother.

My husband and I got married in 2007 and had our boys in 2008 and 2009 and then our stillbirth in 2010. We were so busy and exhausted those first few years of marriage. I will be honest, I was not taking the time to seek the Lord like I knew I should. Weeks would go by without me cracking open my Bible except on Sunday mornings. I realized that I was living off the spiritual life I had during my college days, but it was getting stale.

I wonder if this is a similar struggle for so many young mothers. In the daily demands of young motherhood, we tend to overlook our basic needs, including our spiritual life.

It can feel easy to live off our past spiritual highs or spiritual knowledge. There is definitely grace for young moms, for which I'm extremely grateful. But ultimately our goal as Spirit-filled mothers should be to put our relationship with the Lord first, above and over anything else. Our devotional life might look different in each season of our life, but it should be evident, real and vibrant.

Spirit-filled mothers support their husbands and nurture their marriage relationships.

Elizabeth modeled this kind of commitment to her husband. Together they battled infertility and reproach. She stood by him when he was under the chastening of the Lord. She defended his report of what the angelic messenger had told him. Through it all, her marriage remained a priority.

It's so easy in motherhood to let ourselves go and let our marriages take a back burner. I see so many marriages get distracted by the demands and needs of the kids or the jobs or hobbies. This is a slippery slope, and it's why many empty nesters end up divorcing because they didn't nurture their marriage relationship while they were raising children. I understand the temptation, but we have to work extra hard and be super intentional about making our marriage a priority.

The enemy wants to destroy Christian marriages, and he does it in part through distraction, comparison, contention and busyness. A Spirit-filled mother will recognize that her marriage is a battleground, and she'll fight for it in her prayers and her efforts.

A Spirit-filled mother is sensitive to the Spirit within her, her children and those around her.

Elizabeth recognized that the Spirit had fallen on her and her baby. She saw that He was all over Mary. And she leaned into it. She allowed the Spirit to prophesy and praise through her as she opened her mouth when she greeted Mary. She knew her baby was special and had a significant calling on his life. Elizabeth was discerning and sensitive to the Spirit.

I've heard it said that you know it's the Holy Spirit when you notice that you notice. I love that. When I notice that I notice someone who is hurting, or I notice that one of my kids seems a little more down than usual, or I notice that my husband is overwhelmed—that's what it means to be sensitive to the Spirit.

He will impress truth and knowledge upon us if we're tuned in and listening. Some call it motherly intuition; I call it Spirit-filled motherhood. I want to grow in my discerning spirit, noticing who has needs around me or understanding what God is asking me to say or do in a situation.

Spirit-filled mothers talk publicly and easily about the Lord.

Elizabeth has a couple of moments to shine in this chapter, and every single time, she's talking boldly about the Lord. Whether she's with a dear relative or standing in front of a questioning crowd, she's pointing others to the Lord.

I'm sure we all know women who talk so easily and effortlessly about the Lord every time we're around them. That's the kind of woman I want to be. Our relationship with the Lord doesn't have to be compartmentalized into only church time or our private devotional life. Instead, it should overflow into every interaction and every relationship.

Let's not be afraid to talk about what God is doing in our lives and to praise Him out loud for the big and small things!

Spirit-filled mothers press on even when times are rough.

Elizabeth could have given up on her child-bearing dream, but she continued praying, and God answered her prayer. She could have turned her back on her doubting husband, but instead, she stood closely by his side. She could have been scared about her child's destiny, but instead, she embraced it and supported him.

Motherhood will throw its fair share of challenges our way. I've learned there's no perfect season of motherhood. There are pros and cons to each stage of our children's development. Some stages are harder emotionally while other stages are harder physically. Each transition in and of itself can be difficult. Different children present with varying personalities and struggles. Some have health concerns that baffle and burden us. Bullies, financial worries, our kids' future, rebellion, unwise choices and teenage attitudes—we mothers tend to face the spectrum of rough times as we raise our children.

Spirit-filled mothers will recognize the battle for our children's hearts, and we will fight for truth to win through our prayers and endurance. We aren't given the option to cower away and pretend it will all pass by or that we'll wake up from the nightmare. We press on. We learn to endure.

Spirit-filled mothers speak life over those in their circles.

Many commentators praise Elizabeth for when Mary first walked into her house, thinking about and speaking life over Mary instead of drawing any attention to herself or her own miraculous condition. She thought about Mary's news first and foremost. She was willing to put herself in the background to speak life and blessing over this young mother.

I have been so blessed to have a few mothers in my circle who speak life over me and my calling and successes. In a culture where jealousy and snobby women tend to be the norm, it's so refreshing to find a sisterhood that believes in me and supports me. This is a sign that we are Spirit-filled—that we can speak life, encouragement and blessing over other women and not see their lives as a threat to ours. Moms need encouragement from other moms. I challenge you to find another mom today over whom you can speak a blessing.

Spirit-filled mothers let their children go when God says it's time.

The last verse in chapter 1 says, "And the child continued to grow and to become strong in spirit, and he lived in the deserts until the day of his public appearance to Israel" (Luke 1:80, NASB).

A lot of ground is covered in this verse. It starts with John's child-rearing years and ends with him living alone in the desert as he prepares for his prophetic ministry to Israel. Elizabeth most certainly was involved in the first part of the verse, but where was she when her son left to go live in the wilderness? How did she feel about him leaving? What was her opinion of the type of man he was? (We learn he had quite a radical lifestyle.)

Ultimately, Elizabeth had to let John go so he could fulfill the calling that was on his life. This is never an easy transition for a mother. Thankfully, God prepares us slowly over time as our children need us less and less while they become more and more independent. But the final letting go is a challenge for all of us mothers.

The moment when I'll officially have to let go is looming in my near future with my boys. They are so excited about their futures, and I know I've raised them to be independent men, capable of working hard to provide for a family. Every time they hug me (which I've made a rule has to be at least once a day!), I remind myself to savor their arms around me and my arms around them, knowing someday I'll miss these daily hugs so much. My heart starts to hurt just writing about this day. But I pray I can learn from Elizabeth and allow the Spirit to give me the grace to let go when God says it's time.

Elizabeth makes me want to be a better wife and mother and daughter of the King. Her life challenges me to elevate mine, to let the Spirit have his way in and through me and my children. I'm eternally grateful for the Spirit-filled Elizabeth-type women that God has brought into my life, and I pray I'm able to be that same Elizabeth mentor for others as well.

Heavenly Father, what an amazing woman You showed us through this powerful story of Elizabeth. Thank you for the positive example she is to all of us as mothers. I recognize my inadequacies and beg for your Spirit to fill me completely. I receive the gift of Your Spirit on myself, in my home, and I pray for it to rest on my children. Thank you for the women who have taken an Elizabeth-type interest in my spiritual discipleship; please lead me to younger women whom I can bless and mentor in the same way. In Jesus's name, Amen.

7

MARY

THE MOTHER OF ALL MOTHERS

Shannon Carroll

Mary, the blessed mother of Jesus. What comes to your mind when you are reminded of her and her incredible role in history? If you're like me, you've possibly felt like she's a distant figure to us mortals, an untouchable, a mother unlike any other mother in the history of mothers. And while she was definitely chosen and set apart, I'd like to suggest that we mothers can relate to her more than we ever knew.

I found myself in biblical counseling to work through a traumatic situation that had occurred years prior. I wish I had gotten help sooner before the root of bitterness and the unhealthy patterns had started to fester and putrefy. I couldn't calm my nervous system down and felt like I was in fight or flight constantly, even in my own home—which should be my place of peace and safety. I was easily irritated with those I loved. My energy was tanking. I had no endurance for the demands of life. Headaches were becoming more and more frequent. Everyone in my family was concerned about me and wanted me to get help.

As a type A, driven, motivated, capable individual, being sidelined like this was a hard pill to swallow. I was confused and discouraged. And as a Christian, I was frustrated because I had forgiven—multiple times even. I had been to the altar and made peace with the situation. I thought I was at a place of healing and victorious overcoming only to be triggered again and again, thrown backward in my recovery as I peeled another layer of the trauma and pain. No fun. I wanted off the perpetual rollercoaster.

I am so thankful for a godly, biblical counselor who very quickly assessed one of the root issues causing my continual pain and suffering. And like a good counselor, she didn't tell me what I wanted to hear.

In one session, when I was sharing my deep need to protect my children from experiencing a similar pain and trauma, she so gently, yet pointedly, asked, "Where in God's Word does it say your primary role as a mother is to protect your children?"

Oh no, she didn't! My immediate heart response was, "Excuse me? Don't you go telling me that I can't protect my kids. They're mine! That's *my job* to protect them! Nothing will hurt them on my watch. I'd give my life for them before letting something or someone hurt them!"

She challenged me to spend the week studying mothers in Scripture to find out what our roles are, as designed and designated by God. I guessed this would be an easy lesson, and I'd quickly find justification for my hyper-mother-bear instincts. Surely these maternal impulses were divinely inspired and supported. Right? Boy, was I in for a surprise.

During my Scripture treasure hunt that week, I discovered biblical mothers who birthed children, wept for their children, pleaded with God for their children, provided for their children, and trained and counseled their children. It was a beautiful study, and it gave me such a precious appreciation for the unique role that mothers play in God's perfect design. But nowhere did I find a verse or description detailing that a mother's *primary* duty is to protect her children. Uh oh. I didn't like where this was headed.

As I considered these new insights that week, God gently brought Mary, the mother of Jesus, to my mind. I turned to her story and thought about her for the first time as a real-life mother, not this far-off figure of her that I had built up in my mind. I realized anew that she of all mothers could not protect her Son from harm. She gave the ultimate sacrifice of motherhood—surrendering her Son to ridicule, torture, misunderstanding and even death—so you and I could experience His salvation.

She was fully present at His birth, His growing-up years, His death and later His ascension back to His Heavenly Father. She received and then she gave back. She accepted and then surrendered. She was chosen, and then she had to choose.

I can't even imagine what she went through as a mother.

Her example revealed so clearly to me that I needed to get to a place of surrendering my children back to God instead of relying on my ability to protect them from all harm. Truly, He is the only one who can provide perfect protection—not me. My job is not to hold on to them so tightly that I start to take over the role of God in their life. And yet, this goes against every motherly instinct I have.

We will dive more into this later in the chapter as we tease out the ongoing balance or battle between our motherly nature to protect and God's call to surrender. But for now, let's take a deeper dive into the motherhood journey of Mary. Maybe we will see her in a new light and find fresh hope on our own path of maternal surrender.

WHO IS MARY?

We know Mary as the mother of God (just pause and let the weight and honor of that title sink in for a moment) and yet, she was a woman not unlike you and me.

While she was going about her daily business as a teenage girl, most likely dreaming and preparing for the day when her betrothed, Joseph, would round the corner and commence their wedding, she was approached by an angel. Not just any angel, but one of the top-dog messengers God used to declare history-changing messages to people chosen by God. I can't imagine what that moment must have been like for Mary, but I'm certain she was taken aback. Thankfully, God knows how to address each of us, and He set her mind at ease with these initial words of comfort and greeting,

> Greetings, favored one! The Lord is with you...Do not be afraid, Mary; for you have found favor with God.
> Luke 1:28, 30 (NASB)

Whoa. Her response in verse 29 is probably a vast understatement: "But she was very perplexed at this statement, and kept pondering what kind of salutation this was." No joke!

Initial words in the Scriptures used by herself and others to describe Mary are: virgin, bondslave of the Lord, blessed and favored one.

Mary was human. Mary sinned. Mary had human emotions and fears and joys. And yet she was called out as favored by God. I wonder what her heart was like for God to see and choose her as the one who would carry, birth, counsel and love on His only Son. She had to be pure. She had to have a faith that was extra special. She had to love big.

Though she was favored and chosen for the incredible honor of carrying Jesus, she was entering into a life that would be full of misunderstanding, ridicule and isolation. I'm sure her family didn't believe her report of the divine conception (and I can't say I blame them; that's not a regular occurrence!). I wonder if the stigma of conceiving Jesus "outside of wedlock" stayed with her during her whole life. She suffered in ways we can't imagine as the mother of Jesus, a role that was chosen for her.

Mary and Joseph gave birth to at least six other children (four more boys and at least two girls). Her husband, Joseph, died at some point during Jesus's life before his public ministry. She was involved in Jesus's ministry and was present at His crucifixion.

PROGRESSION OF MARY'S MOTHERHOOD JOURNEY

I remember the very moment when I realized I was going to be a mother. If you're like me, you experienced a wide range of emotions when the reality of pregnancy first hit you—elation, excitement, worry, fear, insecurities, gravity and intense joy. Mommas, from the instant we see a double pink line on the stick until we take our final breath, we are forever changed. Motherhood fundamentally changes each of us.

As soon as David and I cried and rejoiced with our understanding that a new life was growing inside of me, we immediately hopped in the car to go tell our parents. There's something about celebrating the news with others that makes it all the more special and real. My guess is that Mary didn't get the celebration with her family that she so deeply longed for, which is why she ventured to her cousin Elizabeth's house for that connection.

The moment we realize we are carrying something else that is alive inside of us, as women, we begin a transformative shift —to live for our child and not just ourselves. Pregnancy literally changes us from head to toe to heart.

I'm so grateful for a husband who recognizes and even appreciates that I don't have the same body I had when we got married; he knows the changes are because my body went through a complete evolution from years of being pregnant and nursing.

We surrender our bodies, stretch marks and all, for our children. We go through unimaginable pain to bring them into the world. We give up sleep, fun nights out and a clean house so we can provide safe spaces for our children to grow and thrive. No matter how many sacrifices we have to make (or how irritated we may get at our children from time to time), motherhood is a primal joy—a deep calling—for many women.

In a feeble attempt to help us relate to Mary as a mother, let's take a look at the progression of her motherhood journey. Picture her from the lens of a momma as you consider her life's path.

- She was chosen as a teenage girl to be the mother of Jesus.
- After her initial fear and confusion, she responded with a glorious prayer of praise. She gave God glory for the fulfillment of age-old prophecies that the Messiah was coming!
- She gave birth to Jesus in a very humble setting.
- She surrendered and consecrated Jesus, as was the custom, at the temple when he was eight days old.
- She followed her husband's lead and fled with Jesus to Egypt so they'd be protected from Herod's rage.
- She accepted the wise men and their gifts as her only "baby shower."
- She spent years "mommying" Jesus. She nursed Him. She corrected Him (at the temple when he was twelve). She told Him what to do (at the wedding in Cana).
- She pondered all of these things and treasured them in her heart.
- She watched Him suffer and die on the cross.
- She was with the disciples after His reported resurrection, waiting and praying in the Upper Room.

HOW IS MARY LIKE YOU AND ME?

We women can be professional comparers. Within a second of seeing or interacting with another mom, we are already deciding ways we are alike and ways we are different. We measure them out on some random scale—determining in our heart if we are intimidated by or better than or just like another mom. This is an area of our heart where we can each grow as we start to see other moms through the same lens God sees them through. But let's use our professional comparison skills to see how we measure up to and are like Mother Mary.

It's no surprise that you and I were not chosen to bear the divine in our womb! Though we may be proud of our children and honored to be chosen as their mother, only one in all of history was given the title of Mother of Jesus. Because of that distinction, it feels odd to compare Mary to us and our normal lives. She seems so elevated and honored, which she is. Yet, we have to remember her total humanity—and therein we find very special nuggets that can assist us on our motherhood journeys.

Prior to the angel Gabriel's visit, Mary was just a teenage girl. She had plans, dreams and a fiancé. I remember my teenage dreams. In fact, one thing teenage girls do well is dream and fantasize about the future. As a teenager, I was convinced I'd become an obstetrician and travel to Africa to deliver babies in remote villages and tribes. I spent years talking about and preparing for this life calling. I imagined my future husband—tall, dark, handsome. I just knew I'd have at least five kids and at least one daughter. None of my teenage girl dreams came true—well, except for marrying my husband, who is tall, dark and handsome. What do you remember about your teenage dreams and plans?

We can also relate to Mary in that she had friends and family. She grew up in community, and she was especially close to her cousin, Elizabeth. I'm sure she belly laughed with the best of them! I can imagine that some of her family occasionally chewed too loud and got on her last nerve. She sat around the table and enjoyed meals with those she loved.

Mary gave birth to Jesus—and then to at least six other children. Birth seems to be a rite of passage for a woman. Our birth stories can be fun to retell and recount; my boys love hearing about how I threw up twice as my "pushing" phase with Evan, and then he was here. I have birth regrets, as do many women. Knowing what I know now, I'd definitely do things differently. Somehow, whether it's healthy or not, our birth experiences define us and become a deep part of who we are as mothers. Do you wonder how Mary retold Jesus's birth story? What I wouldn't give to hear her version someday.

Mary followed the normal, cultural customs for raising her Son. She took Him to the temple on the eighth day to be circumcised and dedicated. She and Joseph named Him. We have such interesting cultural traditions surrounding pregnancy and birth. I'm honestly glad that we didn't have Pinterest and social media when I was in that stage; I can't imagine the pressure on all the modern-day moms to have the most outlandish gender reveal party, track their baby's progress in every app, get perfect newborn pictures, document every milestone... It's a lot! Yet it's part of our culture, so we jump on the bandwagon. Mary checked all the boxes required of her culturally in raising Jesus.

She had other children. She knew what it was like to be exhausted with multiple children having constant needs. She felt the pressure to make sure everyone had clean clothes and full bellies. I'm sure she refereed a few decent sibling arguments over the years.

Mary was present for big moments in Jesus's life, just like most moms are. We move our schedules around to make room for their school, sports and life events. I feel like I'm a professional taxi driver in our current season of life—with teenage sons who are working and involved in multiple extracurricular activities, yet they aren't old enough yet to have their driver's licenses. It's a busy season. But we as moms show up. We are at the piano recitals and spelling bees and first dances. Mary was at the wedding where Jesus began His earthly ministry. She made being with and around Him a priority— just like we moms do.

And the biggest way I currently relate to Mary is in the example of her being chosen to raise Jesus, yet knowing from the beginning she couldn't hold on to Him forever. She had to give her beloved child back to the Lord, while still showing up as His mother. I can almost feel her tension and this delicate dance she did in her heart every day. As she watched Him grow up, when He was carefree and laughing and playing, she could have so easily wanted to scoop Him up and hold onto Him forever. I believe Mary knew deep down that her ability to protect Jesus was temporary and limited. He wasn't really hers—He was His.

There were times once Jesus started His earthly ministry when she didn't know where He was—or if He was even safe. I'm sure when she heard His cousin, John the Baptist, was jailed for preaching about Jesus, she worried greatly for Jesus. She watched the world love on and embrace Him, and she also witnessed their hatred for her Son.

She was fully His mother, but He wasn't fully hers.

This hits me square between the eyeballs as a mom. I want to save and protect my kids for all time. How would I have responded if I were Mary? Would I have let Him go without a fight? I'm honestly not sure.

HOW IS MARY NOT LIKE YOU AND ME?

Granted, there are many ways we cannot relate to Mary and the life she lived. I absolutely cannot wait to spend some time with her in eternity hearing directly from the source about what life was like as the mother of Jesus. I want to know her hurts, her dreams, the extent of her surrender.

The big, obvious difference is she was chosen to carry the divine in her womb through a supernatural act that I cannot begin to understand. I have questions. And I admire her so much for her surrender and trust in the Lord to let Him accomplish His full will through her —no matter what.

She was approached and spoken to by an angel. And a big-deal messenger at that. Even though angels show up to bring messages to others several times throughout Scripture, we have to acknowledge that this is not a normal, everyday happenstance for most humans. What an experience!

Her divine conception was cause enough for her fiancé, Joseph, to divorce her. What a wild story. Thank God for pairing her with godly, teachable, faith-sensitive Joseph. He believed God and was willing to take a huge risk himself.

She raised Jesus. Have you ever stopped to consider what being Jesus's mom was like? Did He ever cry? Did He think like God when He was five? How does a toddler act if they have no sin in their little-terror hearts? Did He sleep through the night as a newborn? Did He ever roll his eyes as He hit pre-puberty? I'm sure Jesus's childhood was different from any of her other children.

She had the incarnate deity *in and around* her continually. God became man and lived inside her womb. Jesus is and was God and was nursing at her breast. She tucked Him into bed at night, sang songs to Him, fixed Him food—the divine. I wonder if people could sense the Spirit of God when they walked into Mary's house. She was filled with the Spirit of God and interacted with His Spirit daily. What an immense blessing!

The final way we are most unlike Mary is that she was and is revered throughout all of human history. Though some exalt her to sainthood and ultimate perfection, which is not biblical, she did declare that she would be known for all generations.

> For He has had regard for the humble state of His bond-slave; For behold, from this time on all generations will count me blessed.
> Luke 1:48 (NASB)

Her worldwide, eternal fame was birthed in humility and bathed in a surrender that we cannot even begin to imagine or compare ourselves with.

WHAT DOES THIS HAVE TO DO WITH ME?

Maybe you're reading this and having the knee-jerk reaction I had when my counselor proposed the idea that my ultimate job wasn't to protect my kids from all harm. If you're there, then I understand, and there's lots of grace. And I hope you'll hear my heart—our motherly instinct to protect our kids is good. It's what keeps them from falling down the stairs, touching a hot stove, getting into a fight at school or even choosing the wrong mate. We have a special job to help train and protect—no question about it.

The problem comes when we think we can do the best job protecting our kids, and we start to hold onto them ever so tightly as a result. When we don't trust God to ultimately do what is best for and in their lives because we think we can do a better job. That might sound crazy to admit, but I bet deep down we've all had those thoughts.

As with everything in life, there's a delicate balance. For the Christian, the balance is even more important. Yes, we exercise our right and impulse to protect our children from harm. But we realize that ultimately these children belong to God, and He is the ultimate, best protector. We release them back into His hands, trusting that He's a loving Father and can and will do what is best.

There's a tension, but an important one for the Christian momma to work out. Falling into either side of the equation could be detrimental. Caring so much about protecting our kids that we smother them and take the weight of their world on our shoulders is not healthy. And surrendering them to the point of *not caring* or not being involved in any aspect of their life is also not what God is asking of us. I'd like to suggest that this is sometimes a daily thing we lay on the altar, asking God for His Spirit to show us what healthy, surrendered, momma protection looks like for our children for that day.

Thankfully, not all of us have to be like Hannah in the Bible, who vowed to turn her son, Samuel, over to the Lord's work in the temple once he was weaned (1 Samuel 1 and 2).

I cannot even imagine what that sacrifice cost her momma's heart. But her example is one we should all heed, in that we recognize any child we are given is just that—a gift, a gift straight from God.

And we are tasked with the monumental, God-sized responsibility of stewarding that precious life, training it, and protecting it to the best of our ability. Deep, deep down in our hearts we know that the child belongs first to God, so we surrender him or her back to the Lord daily while taking our role as their active momma very seriously and cautiously.

WHAT THEN IS OUR BIBLICAL ROLE AS MOTHERS?

Don't you wish our kids came with an instruction manual and the role of mother came with a solid job description? I can't tell you how many times as a young mom I voiced out loud that I wished God had birthed a unique how-to manual along with my child when they arrived. Especially before they could talk, I just had to guess at what their needs were, using trial and error until we figured it out.

So many of us moms question our ability to responsibly raise our children. Are we doing it right? Are we too strict or too permissive? Should we feed them cereal or avocados first? Will they be okay if we go to church once a week or should we go two? And then we get into the weeds of the "shoulds."

I saw a grief counselor after we experienced our second loss—a stillbirth and then a miscarriage. I remember expressing that I just couldn't go to all the baby showers of my friends and other women in my church. But I struggled because I felt like I "should" go and be there. She so poignantly warned me, "Stop should-ing yourself!" We mommas "should" ourselves to death, always questioning and wondering if we should do more or less or something different altogether.

I find peace in looking at what the Scriptures say the role of mothers "should" be. Let's take a peek at what the Bible says about our extremely important role as mothers.

- We are commissioned to caution and train our children in godly wisdom (Proverbs 1:8-9, Proverbs 22:6, Proverbs 31:1).
- We are called to love our children (Titus 2:4-5).
- Many times in Scripture, motherhood is mentioned in the context of the children's response to their mothers. In fact, this is the most frequent mention of motherhood – that mothers should receive honor, respect and blessing from their children. God reveres mothers and asks that children do the same (Exodus 20:12, Deuteronomy 5:16, Proverbs 31:28).
- Mothers are asked to be self-controlled, pure, managers of the home and kind (Titus 2:4-5).
- We are the carriers of life—what a high honor! The fruit of the womb is described as a reward (Psalm 127:3-5, Psalm 139:13).
- Mothers have a special role to comfort our children and have compassion on them (Isaiah 49:15, Isaiah 66:13).
- We are asked to consider the legacy we can pass down to future generations (2 Timothy 1:5).
- A gift as a mother is to marry, bear children and manage our households (1 Timothy 5:14).
- There are several examples in the Scriptures of mothers pleading for their children's healing, asking God for His best will to be accomplished in their children, and so on (I Kings 3:24-27).

- We can cherish special moments with our children, as Mary did (Luke 2:51).

What a beautiful role we have as mothers! It's actually quite simple; our social media world complicates it and makes us feel like we have to do everything. But this list gives me relief to know what God specifically expects of me as a mother. It's not to be perfect, but it's to love, train, nourish, comfort and plead for my children. I can do that. It's an absolute honor to fulfill that role for the children God has given me.

LETTING GO

We invested in sixteen chickens when our boys were younger, partly so we could always have fresh eggs (there's nothing like a farm fresh egg) but also so the boys could learn to work hard and be responsible. One spring, we didn't catch a broody hen soon enough, so we had to let her sit on the eggs she had collected until they hatched. It was the neatest progression to watch unfold. These momma hens take their instinctive role very seriously.

A few weeks later, the eggs started hatching. And that momma hen immediately stepped into action. Instead of sleeping on top of the eggs as they incubated, now she tucked each tiny chick under her for warmth and protection. The baby chicks felt so comfortable and cared for under their momma. As they got a little older, they'd venture out to explore, always coming right back to the momma. We still enjoy retelling the story of one who hopped on his momma's back and just let her carry him around without a care in the world.

Momma hens have the motherly instinct down pat. When the chicks were old enough to start walking around outside, she'd lead and guide them every step of the way. She let them venture, but she kept a close eye on them. Until one day came when they no longer needed their momma, and she no longer had the impulse to watch over and protect her babies. They were now equals in the herd, each one fending for themselves and going about their own lives.

Watching their progression made me think of my role as a mother. My newborn baby cannot live without me. They are one hundred percent dependent on me to meet their every need and protect them from everything that can harm them. But as our children grow, they need us physically less and less. One day we realize they can go to the potty without momma, they can feed themselves without our help—and we hope and pray they can someday do their laundry without our assistance.

> The progression for us moms is real—and sometimes it's painful to have to let go and let them grow up.

But that's our goal, right, to train them to be independent and responsible adults? It doesn't mean the process is easy or without pain. Each of us as moms has to walk through that series of transitions as we raise our children. Thankfully, there's grace for those of us who are figuring it out. (Ask me how I'm doing when they start driving, though.) And thankfully, God gives us the tool of prayer that can still reach our kids even when they are physically out of our control. Never stop praying for your children, Mommas. It's the greatest gift you can give them, no matter the stage they are in.

JESUS' EXAMPLE

I love that the character of God encompasses the whole person. He truly knows us and can relate to all we are feeling and going through as mothers. In Isaiah 66:13 we see a beautiful expression of God's maternal-type love for His children: "As one whom his mother comforts, so I will comfort you; And you will be comforted in Jerusalem" (NASB).

This describes how many of us mothers feel when we first become mothers—we commit purposely to comforting and protecting our children, just as God committed to that role for His people. But as time and reality come to pass, we start to learn that we can't protect them from everything. At some point, they'll be old enough to make their own decisions, go their own way and experience the consequences of their personal choices.

Jesus expressed this as he mourned the inability to provide perfect comfort and protection to His people:

> Jerusalem, Jerusalem, who kills the prophets and stones those who are sent to her! How often I wanted to gather your children together, the way a hen gathers her chicks under her wings, and you were unwilling.
> Matthew 23:37 (NASB)

The Lord has experienced the same longing we have as mothers, to protect and gather our children so they'll avoid all harm. That's comforting to me. He's also felt what it's like to not be able to provide full protection for them because they rejected Him, and it tore his heart out.

A WORD OF ENCOURAGEMENT

This is a tough lesson to hear and absorb. Whether you are pregnant for the first time, just sent your last kiddo off to college, or are now in the season of gathering at holidays with grandkids—you and I have to realize that our kids are not ours. They are given to us for a season, and as we hold them, we hold them loosely.

I have a teenage son who is set on going to the military and flying fighter planes. Help us, Lord! The more I talk to him about the dangers and harsh realities of this life, the more he seems committed to pursuing it. God has been testing my resolve to perpetually surrender my son and give him back to the Lord. And I understand in my head that the safest place for him to be is in the center of God's will. But my heart hasn't quite caught up.

We have several brave young men and women in our church who have enlisted in the military within the past few years. I've decided that their sacrifice to serve and be willing to give their lives for their country is so immense. Words can't even describe it.

But right behind their sacrifice, is the sacrifice of their momma. I picture moms across our country, knowing every day that their child is following their dream and serving their country—but they as moms have zero control over their child's choices, whereabouts or missions. I imagine the prayers of these mommas are pretty intense at times as they pray their hearts out to the Lord for His protection.

I believe with all my heart that God hears the prayers of mommas and that they reach a special place in His heart.

This is the place you and I need to get to—daily, sometimes moment by moment, in each season and phase of life—carrying our children to the throne of God Almighty, giving them back to Him, asking for His blessing and favor and perfect protection over them. Then when we get up from our prayer time, we have to leave our kids there, trusting that God knows best.

I just want to hug Mary when I see her in heaven. I want to thank her for her incredible sacrifice of loving and nurturing her Messiah-Son and then so beautifully letting Him go. In doing that, Jesus was able to fulfill His eternal destiny of paving the way for my salvation… and the salvation of my precious children.

Heavenly Father, thank you for understanding my concerns and desires as a mother. You know what it's like to long for our children and want the best for them. Thank you for giving our children to us as a gift. I pray we steward any time we have with them—whether they are at home keeping us up at all hours of the night or calling us every few weeks to check in. Help us to embrace our biblical role as their mothers. God, we need Your grace to give our children back to You, to surrender them daily to Your best plan for their lives. "O for grace, to trust You more." Thank you for the example of Mary. Thank you for choosing her to carry your Son, knowing she'd be willing to hold Him loosely so your perfect plan could be accomplished for me and my children. In Jesus's name, Amen.

8

THE CANAANITE WOMAN
THE MOTHER OF FAITHFULNESS

Stephanie Feger

Some moments in life feel fleeting, like snowflakes that serve as a childhood dream for a snow day only to melt upon touching the grass. These moments, while still joyous and meaningful, quickly become forgotten, gone like the wind. Other moments, however, become etched in your subconscious; no amount of willpower can evict them. These moments are like negatives from the film I used as a kid when taking photos. The photograph may go missing, but the negatives are always around, awaiting a trigger to visit a dark room and bring the memory back to life.

While the memories are yours to keep, determining which remains in your easy-to-recall collection and which are tossed away like the weekly garbage is typically beyond your control. Some of the best memories fade without your approval while challenging ones won't budge even if you beg them to. As I look back on my moments, I've found a common thread for the ones that are like temper-tantrum toddlers, refusing to budge, and it's this. If you want a forever memory, roar your loudest momma-bear roar, and it will create lasting effects. Or, find yourself in moments of utter and complete desperation. There, memories are forged in stone in your recollection for life.

I remember all four of my pregnancies; I'm not sure they will ever be forgotten. I can close my eyes and feel all the feels of seeing the pregnancy tests and reexperiencing the tears I shed every time. I can still feel my heart beating extra in anticipation for who was growing hidden in my tummy and the person they were destined to be. But unfortunately, I also remember the worries that accompany each pregnancy. After losing my first child, Faith, through a miscarriage, my following pregnancies came with intense uneasiness.

Would they end in heartache and deep sadness too? Would the pains be the beginning of early labor pains? Would the bleeding be a sign of loss?

When my second child, Eli, was born, I remember him being laid on my chest and heavy sobs escaping my held breath, realizing I had been holding it for nine long, stressful months, fearful I would lose him. Holding my breath was my body's attempt to protect me from the trauma of another loss, and rightfully so since I began preterm labor at twenty-one weeks with him.

A year after his birth, I was blessed with the news of another addition to our family and the unfair pairing of worry followed, especially after the first ultrasound.

My daughter Lyndi's first ultrasound showed an inconsistent heartbeat. I could see her, just as I could her older sister, working so hard to grow and thrive. Even then she was hoping to not let anyone down, her momma included. And, yet, worry wouldn't budge. I was faced with it again, concerned her inconsistent heartbeat could be indicative of news our family wasn't prepared to experience once more.

I fought with God, questioning why He would allow this worry and potential loss again. Hadn't I experienced enough? I gave myself a moment in the car to fall apart, alone, after the news that we would do a repeat ultrasound a few days later to see if her heart had stabilized. I cried. I screamed. I beat on the steering wheel. I felt weak. After that moment of anger, I decided I wasn't giving in or giving up. I was ready to fight. This momma bear was going to do any and everything possible to fight for her baby.

My dad met me at the office of our priest at the time, and as a part of the Catholic faith that I was raised in, myself and my baby experienced the Sacrament of Anointing of the Sick, a sacrament that offered a special healing and blessing. I stood there, shaking with worry and tears, while Fr. Scott put holy oil on my forehead and prayed over my body, my heart and my baby. I made a promise to God that day that if this baby made it, I'd make sure he or she knew Him. (The truth is, I would have followed through on my end of the bargain even if it felt like He hadn't.)

When I walked out of the church, I also made a pact to pray like it was going out of style. Any time I worried, I traded it in for prayer. At the time, conversational prayer was challenging for me. I honestly didn't even know how to do it. My God was amazing, but He seemed far away, and words didn't seem worthy enough. So I resorted to the one prayer I committed to muscle memory: The Lord's Prayer (otherwise known as The Our Father). Every mass I attended we'd always say it together as a congregation, so I knew it by heart. It was what I prayed every time I got in an airplane and my fear of heights took over. And, while my fear was a bit different this time, I knew that prayer would get me through like it always had in the past.

Our Father, who art in heaven, hallowed be thy name. Thy Kingdom come, thy will be done, on earth as it is in Heaven. Give us this day our daily bread and forgive us our trespasses. As we forgive those who trespass against us, lead us not into temptation and deliver us from evil. Amen.

Those days between my first ultrasound and second, this prayer was on repeat like a broken record. Over and over again, I would declare it to God, in my thoughts and aloud where possible. The world moved fast around me, so when I was talking with others and going about my day, it was easier to shift my focus onto other things. But there was one part of my day that felt isolating, lonely even. When I went to the bathroom, I was terrified.

I spotted during my pregnancy with Faith. In fact, my spotting was the first sign of my miscarriage with her. When I was pregnant with Eli, I also spotted. I couldn't walk one lap around the neighborhood without spotting and beginning contractions, so much so that the labor and delivery nurses got to know me quickly for the number of times my spotting brought me into the hospital. So my fear of the bathrooms was real and rational.

Every time I needed to go—which is a lot as a pregnant woman—I dreaded the potential of seeing blood. But I was determined to trade worry for prayer. I would begin praying the Our Father as I walked into the bathroom. Depending upon my worry capacity for the day, sometimes I would make it through the whole prayer and repeat it time and time again until I made it out of the bathroom unscathed. Other times, I could get hung up on one verse of it, and I said it on repeat. Either way, I prayed.

Every. Single. Time.

And I didn't stop praying when the news of the second ultrasound was favorable. I didn't stop when the spotting and preterm labor did come. I didn't stop when I could feel her move or when I couldn't. I didn't stop until I held her in my arms, and then I picked up new prayers and resorted back to that old reliable when my fourth and final pregnancy with Luke had similar worries. This memory of my desperate, relentless praying is a moment I'll always remember. And it is a moment that I recalled as I read the story of the Canaanite woman found in Matthew 15.

Leaving that place, Jesus withdrew to the region of Tyre and

Sidon. A Canaanite woman from that vicinity came to him, crying out, "Lord, Son of David, have mercy on me! My daughter is demon-possessed and suffering terribly."

Jesus did not answer a word. So his disciples came to him and urged him, "Send her away, for she keeps crying out after us."

He answered, "I was sent only to the lost sheep of Israel." The woman came and knelt before him. "Lord, help me!" she said.

He replied, "It is not right to take the children's bread and toss it to the dogs."

"Yes it is, Lord," she said. "Even the dogs eat the crumbs that fall from their master's table."

Then Jesus said to her, "Woman, you have great faith! Your request is granted." And her daughter was healed at that moment.
Matthew 15:21-28 (NIV)

Talk about a momma bear. The Canaanite woman was one. No doubt about it. She defied cultural expectations and norms. She fought hard for her daughter. She was deep in the face of crisis. And she did what many of us mothers possibly need a reminder to do when it's tough: She had a faith that wouldn't stop.

FINDING FAITH IN THE FACE OF DOUBT

Before we should go much further, it's important to note just who this woman was. Although we have very few verses in Scripture on her—seven verses in Matthew 15 and another six verses in Mark 7 —we know a lot about her from the additional context the two Gospel writers offer.

While we are given no name for her, we do know that this mother was a Canaanite. In Mark, she's described as a Syrophoenician, meaning she was Greek and born in Syrian Phoenicia. I did more research to understand her a bit more, knowing that nothing in Scripture should be overlooked; it all has meaning.

Being a Canaanite was as much a heritage as it was a culture. It was something she was born into and a community she was actively a part of. It wasn't something she just had—like being a brunette or owning the fact that she's of average height. Instead, it was a part of her identity, much like being Christian is to us today.

Knowing this about her, we also know that she was not Jewish; in fact, Canaanites were considered enemies of Israel.[1] Israelites worshiped one true God; Canaanites worshiped many gods. We've heard the word Canaan before in Scripture, as far back as Genesis 9, when Noah was angry at the behavior of his son, Ham, after finding Noah drunk and naked. From this lack of respect, Noah cursed Ham by cursing his son, Canaan. "Cursed be Canaan! The lowest of slaves will he be to his brothers" (Genesis 9:25, NIV).

These Canaanites were descendants of Canaan, and this woman was likely similar to the rest of the people in her culture. She was a pagan living in a culture that glorified polytheism. Jesus was not to her what he was to others. In her culture, he was an enemy; someone who went completely against the belief system she was taught.

But momma bears don't always work within strict boundaries. When it comes to caring for our children, we go to great measures, this Canaanite woman included.

And, Jesus goes to great measures too. Don't let it be lost in this story of faith how Jesus was where he was supposed to be when he was supposed to be there. His ministry was coming to a close; his death was drawing near. He was heading toward Jerusalem, and Matthew 15:21 notes this: "Leaving that place, Jesus withdrew to the region of Tyre and Sidon." This was Canaanite territory. Jesus knew that a teaching moment was to come—both for a mother who would do anything for her child and his disciples.

We don't know how the Canaanite woman found Jesus. He had retreated to a private house and was hoping to be alone for a bit. But she didn't care of His wants; she had an agenda and finding Him was a part of it.

Imagine for a moment what you would do (or have done) for the sake of your children. I had an out-of-body experience once when I observed a bully speak lies to my kids. Words and phrases I hadn't even previously thought came forth, making it clear that bully behavior wouldn't be tolerated. When my son slipped on creek rocks covered in moss and began rolling like a limp log in a river, my motherly instinct moved my legs despite my logical brain saying it was a cold winter day in an attempt to fish my son out of the water's hold. My voice hits new heights when my kids are on the basketball courts, allowing them to hear my cheers begrudgingly, no matter where they are on the floor. And, like the Canaanite woman, when something isn't right with my children, I will do anything to seek help. Anything.

In her pursuit to do anything, she gained everything.

She was a woman who was born into a culture that doubted. She was a woman who lived a life different from those she despised. And yet, through the doubt was a seed of faith. Just a few chapters later in Matthew, Jesus tells us this: "Truly I tell you, if you have faith as small as a mustard seed, you can say to this mountain, 'Move from here to there,' and it will move. Nothing will be impossible for you" (Matthew 17:20, NIV).

Her faith through doubt made her body lift from grieving over her demon-possessed daughter and walk to find Jesus. Her faith through doubt took her searching for who knows how long to who knows where to find the one she had heard could heal. Her faith through doubt pushed her through immobilization, charging her to not give up until she tried everything—Jesus included—to save her daughter.

When I was in high school, I had the best religion teacher. I could go on and on about how she shaped my faith, but one thing she told our class once stuck with me like gum does to a shoe. "All doubt isn't bad," she shared. "Constructive doubt is the type of doubt that leads us to greater truth." The Canaanite woman must have believed. Her faith might have been as small as a mustard seed, but it was her constructive doubt that found her faith and, when paired with her willingness to try everything including a meeting with Jesus, her daughter was healed.

LEADING WITH FAITH THROUGH COUNTLESS OBSTACLES

We know that the Canaanite woman knew who Jesus was by what she said. In Matthew 15, she refers to Jesus as Lord three times, each time she speaks to Him. But what's even more interesting is how she refers to Him the first time: "Lord, Son of David, have mercy on me!" (Matthew 15:22, NIV) Son of David is a title referencing the lineage of David reserved for the Jewish Messiah, a Messiah Canaanites didn't believe in. Yet, she comes to Jesus with reverence, persistence and humility.

How does Jesus respond? Well, not in typical Jesus fashion, that's for sure.

The Jesus I know is loving. He's the one who sees people; like really sees them. He's the one who goes after a single lost sheep willingly and with a fervent commitment. He's the one who laughs with children and always finds time for people. My Jesus is compassionate, empathetic and probably was like my husband's grandmother, who gave those lasting hugs that you couldn't break free from (and never wanted to anyway). I could never have imagined my Jesus would have done what Scripture tells us He did next.

"Jesus did not answer a word."
Matthew 15:23 (NIV)

Nothing. After the Canaanite woman trekked away from her baby, hiked only God knows how many miles and hills, likely staked out to see where Jesus went and then humbly cried out to Him for mercy and begging for healing of her daughter who was terribly suffering, Jesus. Said. Nothing.

Scripture doesn't tell us anything more than the fact that He didn't speak a word, but I can only imagine what He spoke without words. Actions speak louder than words, right? What were Jesus's nonverbal cues like? Did His eyes have the loving gaze that I dream about? Or did He have His arms crossed in annoyance? Did He not have the ability to say a word because He wasn't given any time? Immediately following this in Scripture, we're told that His disciples came to Jesus and urged Him to shoo her away. Maybe He didn't say a word because His disciples piped in first.

"Send her away, for she keeps crying out after us."
Matthew 15:23 (NIV)

Oh, to be a fly on the wall for this conversation. I'd love to have the ability to pause this scene in time and look at it from all angles and have an insider peek into the unique thoughts of each person in the room. Jesus was probably exhausted, and the disciples were too. He knew what was to come and, in the midst of it, knew that He needed to teach His disciples to continue His life-changing and life-giving work soon.

The disciples were probably feeling a bit like Jesus's bodyguards, wanting to keep Him safe and frustrated that a woman who didn't even believe would waste their time. And this desperate mother would do anything to save her baby, even if it meant going against everything she thought was true.

The Canaanite woman, however, had faith despite her obstacles. She had likely pushed through cultural obstacles and physical obstacles to get to this place. And she wasn't planning on giving up soon. Not answering isn't the same as a "no." And even at the begging of

Jesus's disciples, she wasn't going to leave without falling to her knees and begging more.

As the story continues in Matthew 15, she faces more obstacles. Jesus reminds her who He came here for. "He answered, 'I was sent only to the lost sheep of Israel.'" Don't you remember, woman? Jesus came for your enemies.

Not a big enough obstacle for her. "The woman came and knelt before him. 'Lord, help me!' she said."

Jesus then referred to the Canaanites as dogs and the Israelites as children. "He replied, 'It is not right to take the children's bread and toss it to the dogs.'"

And she didn't take the bait. She wasn't leaving; she'd made it this far. Her everything was on the line. And it paid off. "'Yes it is, Lord,' she said. 'Even the dogs eat the crumbs that fall from their master's table.' Then Jesus said to her, 'Woman, you have great faith! Your request is granted.' And her daughter was healed at that moment."

Jesus seemingly ignored her. Jesus' disciples begged for Him to send her away. Jesus stated what all believed: that He came for the Israelites, God's chosen people. Jesus questioned if bread (his healing salvation) should be taken from His people for her.

And through all of this, Jesus wasn't just speaking; He was listening. He was watching. He was teaching.

Where others would see obstacles, she saw opportunities. Others (sometimes ourselves included) give up when the going gets hard. But this mother held on with all her strength. She wasn't budging until Jesus heard her heart's plea. And, friend, He did and always does.

EMBRACING A FAITH IN CRUMBS

Crumbs. My van seems to be one big, massive one. During this season of my life—where my three kids are between eight and twelve years old and always on the go (and always eating in the van) —I fear looking under car seats, under floor mats or in any cubby for fear of what I'll find.

Recently on the way to church, my youngest, Luke, yelled in joy from the second row. "Yes! Look what I found. I'm so lucky." I cringed, unsure of what exactly he would find. It's always questionable. A dime was his treasure, not mold from a french fry he was hoarding for a rainy day. Praise God! (And lucky him, the dime was on heads!)

But in truth, I'd give anything for a weekly van cleaning, because I think I have enough crumbs in my vehicle to feed our family of five for a day, maybe longer. I used to be embarrassed by this (who am I kidding, I still am), but I also know that this season won't last. Crumbs will diminish, and so will car trips with the kids telling me of their days, their woes and their questions. I would love to wish away the former but never the latter.

Just the other day I was sitting in the carpool pickup line when my stomach growled. Apparently, I had forgotten to scarf a lunch that day, and my belly wanted to remind me. I rolled my eyes; everything seemed to want my attention nowadays, bellies included. So, I went on the hunt for something to shut it up. Surely we had a mint stashed somewhere. In my search, I uncovered a nearly-eaten peanut butter and chocolate breakfast bar. I wish I could blame my kids for this, but it was mine. My stomach was grateful for my forgetfulness, even if all that was left were just some crumbs. The crumbs would suffice, and they did.

As I studied the Canaanite woman, I came across several sermons from others who spent time trying to understand the hardest part of this story to swallow; the part where Jesus talks about children's bread and dogs and the Canaanite woman mentions crumbs.

> He replied, "It is not right to take the children's bread and
> toss it to the dogs."
> Matthew 15:26 (NIV)

To understand this portion of Scripture, we need to do some
dissecting.

- First up, let's talk about bread. Jesus isn't asking the
  Canaanite woman a literal question. He isn't wondering if
  her being there meant that some children somewhere
  wouldn't get bread for dinner that night. Instead, His
  statement refers to a different type of belly-rumbling
  satisfaction: Him.
- The children he references are the Canaanites' enemies. In
  Matthew 15:24 Jesus states that He was sent only to the lost
  sheep of Israel. While this situation pushes the envelope on
  this statement, it reminds us that Jesus was the Messiah the
  Jews had been waiting for. God's children were the
  Israelites.
- Throughout Scripture, bread is a constant. In Exodus, we
  are taught about how we shouldn't hoard manna; we will
  get our day's fill. Jesus broke bread with His disciples and
  used three loaves to help feed thousands. In all cases, while
  bread is body-filling, it's a symbol of the soul-giving bread
  that Jesus is for us.
- If you have a dog, you know that they are persistent
  beggars. Waiting at your feet each meal, they would give
  anything for the scraps. Even trained dogs will sneak a
  forgotten leftover if their owners aren't looking. When Jesus
  refers to dogs here, He isn't calling her one. Instead, He's
  referencing those who are waiting and watching, just like
  she is.

With this context in mind, Matthew 15:26-27 takes on a different
perspective. When we remember that Jesus's disciples are with him,
we are reminded that this is a learning opportunity for them as well.

The Jesus I know probably had a kindness and gentleness to his statement, encouraging the Canaanite woman to confidently reply as she did. Her answer is everything.

> "Yes it is, Lord," she said. "Even the dogs eat the crumbs
> that fall from their master's table."
> Matthew 15:27 (NIV)

The Canaanite woman was wise. Or maybe in her desperation, she was willing to take anything. Maybe she's like those who are willing to give *anything* to shake the hand of their favorite celebrity. Just a crumb will do, Lord. That was her answer.

She didn't need everything; she just needed a crumb. She knew that a crumb of Jesus's promise could heal her daughter. Just like a cookie crumb, all the ingredients it takes to fulfill us can be found in a single crumb.

She didn't need the whole loaf of bread; she'd happily settle for a single, powerful, healing crumb.

Faith the size of a mustard seed and that of a crumb is all that is needed. And in times of desperation, we may feel like all we have to give are prayers in the size of crumbs. Through our tears, we may only be able to cry out words that feel like crumbs. But God doesn't answer us in hidden crumbs found in vans; He answers us in loaves of bread. All He asks for is our faith, even if crumbs are all we have the ability to offer.

"WOMAN, YOU HAVE GREAT FAITH! YOUR REQUEST IS GRANTED!"

Imagine the look on her face when the Canaanite woman heard Jesus's words. If she was anything like me—in that I carry no poker face—you could likely read her feelings without her needing to speak a word. Relief. Joy. Gratitude. Belief. Awe. These are some feelings I suspect she held all at once as she ran back to her home to see that, in fact, her daughter was healed. Mark 7:30 says: "She went home and found her child lying on the bed, and the demon gone" (NIV).

Because of her faithfulness, her daughter was healed. Because of her constructive doubt, her daughter would experience life again. Because she jumped through hurdles instead of seeing them as obstacles, her daughter likely learned of the power of Jesus. Because of crumbs, her and her daughter's lives were forever changed.

We may not be Canaanites, but we aren't too different from this woman. We have our own doubts. Even those of us who are confident in our Savior find ourselves questioning when our prayers feel like they are being ignored. We understand the great lengths this mother would go to when her daughter was held captive by demons. We will do the same for our kids, who are coerced by society's lies. And yet, we forget the power of a crumb.

Embrace that momma bear energy.

When crises arise—and, Momma, they will—consider the all-too-familiar phrase we've lived before: fight, flight or freeze. In the world of psychology, immobilization can happen in crisis. Some of us freeze, unable to do anything. Others run from it, hoping it will forget about us while we try to forget about it. And, others fight through it. Instead of using your fists for fighting, put them together and pray through it.

The Canaanite woman is living proof of the power of intercession prayer. As mothers, we felt like we could keep our babies safe in utero. We know the power of momma kisses on boo-boos. But when the hardships get bigger and harder, let's not forget who does the real healing: God. Momma, you can't fix everything. And, actually, you can't fix anything. But I know someone who can: God. When you pray for your kids, God listens.

Jesus is for all of us, friends and foes alike.

Jesus knew He could meet this woman in His little detour to enemy territory. He knew behind that tough exterior was a woman who believed, or at least wanted to. And He also wanted to remind those around Him—His best buddies included—that He wasn't just for those who believed. He came for all. He is accessible to all. He is Savior to any and everyone who puts their faith in Him.

Jesus came for me. He came for you. He came for those we love and for those we have a hard time loving. He came for those who know Him and those who have yet to hear His name. He came for the believers and those who have yet to believe. He came for those who live their life for Him and those who are wayward, in hopes that they will find the narrow path. He came for us all.

Eyes are watching, then and now.

Jesus had disciples watching His every move. They were learning alongside Him daily. And yet, they were tired too. They were annoyed with this woman and wanted her gone. What a teachable moment Jesus had. And, as you would have guessed, Jesus doesn't let a teachable moment pass Him up. He would of course use it.

You have little eyes watching too. They see how you navigate hardships and celebrate successes. They see you struggle, and in your hardships, they learn how to navigate their hardships later. If you fight with your words, they notice. And, if you fight on your knees in prayer, they notice that too. Never neglect the fact that you have the power and the charge to teach your kids.

> *Our Father, who art in heaven, hallowed be thy name. Thy Kingdom come, thy will be done, on earth as it is in Heaven. Give us this day our daily bread and forgive us our trespasses. As we forgive those who trespass against us, lead us not into temptation and deliver us from evil. Amen.*

Momma, your faith becomes a seed of faith in the minds and hearts of your children. It is like daily bread that nourishes you and offers a crumb to those around you. If you want to ensure your children have the muscle memory to fight hardships, be like the Canaanite woman and have faith through doubt, refuse to let obstacles stop you and be grateful for any and all crumbs.

───────

Heavenly Father, help me to have the persistence, faithfulness and gratitude that the Canaanite woman showed. In a world that seeks a whole loaf, remind me that a crumb is all I need, and a mustard seed is all You request. I pray, Lord, that when I feel overwhelmed by hardships my kids endure, I turn to You with utmost perseverance, knowing that You hear my prayers for my children, and You have the power to answer. In Jesus's name, Amen.

9

YOU, THE MOTHER OF...

Wow, Momma! We have been on quite the journey together, haven't we?!

When we embarked on this book journey studying eight biblical mothers, we knew we'd walk away with new insights on how we could grow as mothers. What we didn't expect was how blown away we would be by the richness and relevance of Scripture for us as mothers in today's world. While so much seems to have changed since these ancient stories were recorded, we are reminded that so, so much has remained the same, motherhood struggles included.

Truly almost every angle of motherhood can be found in these pages. And hopefully you've gained a new respect for these biblical mothers who have shown us how to love, pray, surrender and train our children—and any children we get the opportunity to mentor and lead—in the ways of the Lord. This is no small calling, Momma, but God's given you the skills to conquer anything through Him.

Our prayer is that our insights have inspired (and challenged) you as you walk through motherhood—today and throughout the varying stages to come. No one's path is alike, and none of us have mothered perfectly. We all fail. We all have regrets. But our intent through this deep dive is for you to experience grace, joy and energy for the task at hand.

Any time you have heard the voice of condemnation or accusation, please know that voice is from the enemy and not from the Lord. God convicts us but does not condemn us. He challenges us to grow and mature, but not through the methods of shame and guilt. We all have maturing to do in the way we approach motherhood; sanctification is a life-long process.

Each of the eight amazing women we studied has spoken to us in unique ways. Their example from centuries ago lives on and impacts us in our current, modern-day life right this very second. This is an incredible, supernatural phenomenon.

As you close this book (and maybe consider gifting it to a friend or using it in your next small group Bible study), we want to make sure you have let the truths sink deep in your heart and impact the way you think and act as a mother. Biblical stories are not just for our entertainment; they're for our edification. Through these sometimes-obscure women, we can experience life-changing encounters.

So we have a challenge for you! Spend some moments in your quiet time considering each of these mothers and how you can allow her example to create a tangible response in your life. These questions might provide helpful journal prompts for you as you internalize the lessons from these eight mothers.

SARAH, THE MOTHER OF PATIENCE

What parts of your motherhood journey are you feeling a bit impatient with? Are you desiring to become a mother but struggling with the limitations you feel your body is experiencing? Or are you always wishing the next phase of motherhood would arrive too quickly? Have you been praying to God for help and feel a bit like His return reply is a tad delayed?

Consider Sarah's long wait. Remember how God views time (unfortunately and fortunately it's not how we do). Reflect on how you can see God working in your waiting, because we promise you, He is. Our challenge to you is to change your laugh from laughter found in uncertainty and disbelief or laughter in the face of one's enemy to laughter in relishing the beautiful joy of God's promises. God will answer your prayers, Momma. He promises.

HAGAR, THE MOTHER WHO WAS SEEN

Do you feel like a mother on the run? Want to hop on a cruise ship with no end destination or move to Hawaii and change your name? (Don't fret, we have had these thoughts before ourselves too.) Have you felt taken advantage of, not heard, used and abused, uncared for? Do you feel like God sees others around you but chooses to not look your way? Feel like you are meandering through the wilderness without a purpose or a plan?

Hagar felt all those feelings, and in the middle of her despair, she was gifted with a divine appointment: an angel of the Lord encounter. While the message wasn't exactly what she hoped for (and, let's be honest, God doesn't always answer our prayers how we'd initially prefer), she felt seen. So much so that she named God the God Who Sees. Never forget that God sees you; all of you. And He loves you too.

JOCHEBED, THE MOTHER OF COURAGE

Ever second-guessed if you should have brought children into this chaotic world? Are you in the thick of questioning that right this very moment? Are you worried about how this broken world may impact your beautiful child? Worried that your positive influence will be trumped by society's negative one? Are you tired and weary, Momma?

Jochebed was too, and yet, she's living proof that when the going gets tough, we find a way. That way may not be our first choice, but

God is working in and through it. As long as He is our way, good will come. We need to be in community with other witnesses, get our hearts focused on what matters most, actively choose to endure despite obstacles and fix our eyes on Jesus. The road will be rocky, but the end destination is worth it. And, rest assured, you aren't doing this alone. Not now; not ever.

BATHSHEBA, THE MOTHER OF WISDOM

Are you carrying the weight of another person's sin? Is the scarlet letter heavy, unfair and unwarranted, but you're stuck with it anyway? Feeling judged and ashamed by others who misunderstand and wrongfully accuse? Are you in a place in life you didn't plan for, you didn't ask for, you didn't desire but feel determined to see through? Are you searching for silver linings amid a tapestry of frayed edges?

Bathsheba wore her scarlet letter with grace. Despite being undeserving of the probable gossip and shame thrown her way, she chose to follow God anyway and learned from her situation. In doing so, she broke through generational curses and you can too, Momma. Don't feel stuck in your situation; realize God has the power to use your circumstances for good if you let Him.

THE SHUNAMMITE WOMAN, THE MOTHER OF CONTENTMENT

Are you weighed down by sorrow? Do you find it hard to stop the waterworks, believe good can come from your situation and see the light at the end of the tunnel? Are you in the pit of despair, having a tough time finding a rope to pull yourself out of it? Does every step in life feel challenging, the worries of the world heavy on your shoulders?

The Shunammite Woman was there, and yet in her darkest moment, she rested in Him and left the rest to Him. Her charge was to make room for God. Check. His charge was to not break His promise. Check. Create a space for God in your life, and He will bless you beyond measure. Stop trying to weave your own ladder from the rope you go looking for. Instead, reach out your hand, Momma. God's got a rope within arm's reach to pull you through. All *is* well.

ELIZABETH, THE MOTHER OF GRACE

Have you experienced deep brokenness and are seeking ways to bind up your wounds? Do you have feelings of unworthiness and not being enough? Do you feel the world moving fast, leaving you behind in the process? Do your broken pieces feel too fractured to put back together? Are you finding it hard to find hope?

Elizabeth understood brokenness deeply and yet, she is also a walking testament to God creating broken to beautiful stories. He did it for her; He'll do it for you too. Stop trying to write your own story, Momma. Hand over the pen; let God become your life's author. His story is better than the one you could ever write for yourself anyway. Spirit-filled motherhood awaits if you'll find that place of sweet surrender.

MARY, THE MOTHER OF ALL MOTHERS

Are you a helicopter mom, trying to coordinate every move of your child for fear of them getting hurt, failing at something or missing an opportunity? Do you find it hard to balance your motherly instinct to protect with God's call for you to surrender all? Be honest with yourself. Do you think you can better care for your children than God can? (And while your answer is likely no, do your actions align accordingly?)

Imagine the worries Mary, the mother of Jesus, had mothering the Son of God. If she can surrender her child to God, surely we can. We are called to help protect our children, absolutely. But our children really aren't ours; they are God's. He gives them to us on loan. He just entrusted us to care for them while they are here. God is the ultimate protector, and He asks us to merely trust Him. Can you let go and let God?

THE CANAANITE WOMAN, THE MOTHER OF FAITHFULNESS

Are you willing to do anything, right here and right now, for your child? Is your momma bear on high alert? Are you begging God for His intervention in your child's life? What are you willing to do when the going gets tough? Better question, who will you turn to?

The Canaanite woman was willing to do anything for her everything. Saving her daughter became her mission; seeking a mere crumb from Jesus was her end goal. It was her faith that saved her daughter. Your faith has the power to save your children too. In a world where momma bears fight for injustices, stand up for their children and are willing to do any and everything to get what their children deserve, we challenge you to fight not with your hands or your voice but on your knees through prayer and petition. All you need is a crumb, Momma. Just a tiny crumb.

It's time to decide who *you* are as a mother. Or better yet, who *you* want to be.

What will your legacy be and what will you pass on to future generations? Maybe you'll be the Mother of Prayer, the Mother of Hospitality, the Mother of Laughter. Will your children and grandchildren remember you as the Mother of Possibility or the Mother of Encouragement?

No matter your age or motherhood stage, no matter your financial position or your disposition, you are making a difference for eternity in your God-given calling and role as a mother. The world is grateful for your influence.

WE'RE HERE FOR YOU

Your story isn't finished; it's likely just begun.

God doesn't create broken-to-beautiful stories overnight. Instead, He refines you while He redeems you, and, Momma, this takes time. While you may feel like time is of the essence (and it is), life isn't about seeking a destination (although we know where we have our eyes set). Instead, it's about the journey to get there. And God uses every step of your journey—every crossroad, detour, twist and turn —to help you fulfill your calling.

God has a plan for you, and motherhood may be a large part of it. As you review the lives of these biblical mothers and reflect on your own story of redemption, consider how He is helping you impact the next generation, leave the world better than you found it and draw more people to Him in the process.

To assist you on your own broken-to-beautiful motherhood journey, we wanted to offer you some additional resources we've found helpful in ours.

DOWNLOAD SCRIPTURE REFERENCES AND JOURNAL PROMPTS

If there is one piece of advice we are confident will help you on any journey you take—motherhood included—it's to be in the Word daily. The Bible is living and breathing, begging to be a part of your life in ways you couldn't dream possible. But the only way for it to change you is for you to make a commitment to crack open its spine, rest in the messages found on each page and receive the truth God has for you. We've seen how Scripture has changed us; we are excited to learn how it will continue to change you.

As you study these eight women alongside us, we want you to dig into each woman's story in Scripture as well. Wrestle with their stories. Put yourself in each woman's shoes. Walk a day in her life. Consider how her story applies to yours. Study her deeply like we have, and we know God will show up for you and in you. While specific Scripture verses used as a part of our individual studies are acknowledged in each chapter, we figured you'd find it helpful to have them listed in one place along with journal prompts to support your personal study time.

We encourage you to visit www.BrokenandBeautifulPress.com to download journal prompts and Scripture passages to align with each chapter of this book.

CONTINUE TO LEARN ALONGSIDE US

Finally, we'd love to personally invite you to connect with us, join our community and deepen your faith alongside us. We believe in the power of sisterhood, and we've seen how community changes people, broken and beautiful women included. Here are a few ways we can stay in touch!

Tune into the Broken & Beautiful Podcast.

The Broken & Beautiful Podcast offers Scripture-based and Spirit-led discussions on relevant topics Christian women experience and real-time biblical insights for life-changing application. We invite you to specifically carve out time to enjoy the Women of Redemption series of the podcast, which highlights seven broken and beautiful stories of women in the Bible, some of which are found in this book and others that aren't, including Hannah, Ruth, Eve, the woman caught in adultery, and the woman with the issue of blood. What a beautiful complement to the messages you've just read.

Join our email list.

Visit www.BrokenandBeautifulRetreats.com to join our email list, where you'll be among the first to know of upcoming retreats, new blog posts, ways to bring broken and beautiful experiences to your community and more. Enjoy our inspiration emails and journal prompts, as well.

Follow us on Facebook and Instagram and visit our YouTube channel.

We love connecting with other Christian women and offering ongoing inspiration on social media. We are active on Facebook and Instagram and have a growing YouTube channel that we think you'll find meaningful.

AN INTERACTIVE BIBLE STUDY ON MOTHERHOOD

Never underestimate the power of influence a mother has over her children. In fact, a Christian mom is one of the most powerful forces on earth!

Any child we are given is just that—a gift straight from God. While we know this, it's hard to live this truth daily. As a companion study to *Women of Redemption: Motherhood Wisdom from 8 Biblical Matriarchs*, we are giving you the opportunity to invite the stories of eight biblical mothers into your personal or group Bible study time to discover the mother you are called to be and the mother you desire to become.

Being a Christian mother is one of the most important roles any woman will ever have. But it is also one of the most challenging. Rewarding and overwhelming can be found in the same sentence when motherhood is spoken of, just ask a mother or take a moment to reflect on your own motherhood story. In this Bible study, you'll be able to dive deep into the lives of broken to beautiful women found in Scripture who exemplified what it means to be a godly mother. Through their stories of faith, surrender, perseverance and grace, timeless lessons are uncovered to help equip you—a mother of today—for your journey ahead.

Authors Shannon Carroll and Stephanie Feger share their personal motherhood stories alongside the biblical accounts of Sarah, Hagar, Jochebed, Bathsheba, Mary, Elizabeth, the Shunammite woman and the Canaanite woman. Noting the triumphs and hardships faced by each, they mine Scripture and listen to God's messages in their own parenting experiences to uncover powerful insights for mothers navigating worry, fear, regret and the unique demands of raising children for God's purposes in today's culture.

Through daily reflections, additional Scripture insights, group discussion questions, prayer prompts and more, this interactive Bible study is designed for individual or group use, to challenge, inspire and offer practical application for mothers of all types. Women aspiring to motherhood, mothers in the trenches of raising the next generation and matriarchs who seek to offer mentorship to other mothers will be strengthened and set free through this Bible study to fully live out their sacred calling, right where God has them each day.

Learn more at www.BrokenandBeautifulPress.com. The *Women of Redemption: An Interactive Bible Study on Motherhood* is expected to release Fall 2024.

RESOURCES

GOD LOVES MOTHERS

1. *Statistics About Mothers Around the World.* Sound Vision, 2024. https://www.soundvision.com/article/statistics-about-mothers-around-the-world

1. SARAH

1. The Bible Answer, 2014. https://thebibleanswer.org/most-mentioned-woman-in-bible/
2. YouVersion is my favorite!
3. Blue Letter Bible. https://www.blueletterbible.org
4. Ellis, Marian Jordan. *Portrait: Sarah, Women of the Bible.* YouTube, 2019. https://www.youtube.com/watch?v=BUAZmLyzXNo

2. HAGAR

1. Farlx International. *The Farlex Idioms and Slang Dictionary.* (2017)
2. Abarim-Publications.com, *Hagar Meaning.* (2006) https://www.abarim-publications.com/Meaning/Hagar.html
3. National Sexual Violence Resource Center (NSVRC), 2024. www.NSVRC.org/statistics

4. BATHSHEBA

1. Ellis, Linda. *The Dash: Making a Difference With Your Life* Simple Truths; New edition. (January 1, 2017)

5. THE SHUNAMMITE WOMAN

1. Bible Study Tools. Easton, Matthew George. *Entry for Shunem*, Easton's Bible Dictionary. https://www.biblestudytools.com/dictionary/shunem/
2. Bible Tools, 1992-2024. https://www.bibletools.org
3. Destination Church. *Lessons from the Shunammite Woman.* (2019) https://www.youtube.com/watch?v=i4YeA0Bd-Ko
4. Furtick, Steven. *There's More to the Story*, Elevation Church. (2016) https://youtu.be/6a1p1_jzM14?si=FHmWUugDuOJVv2Fy

8. THE CANAANITE WOMAN

1. Mark, Joshua J. *Canaan Definition*. World History Encyclopedia (2018) https://www.worldhistory.org/canaan/

ACKNOWLEDGMENTS

We both had a reason to not attend the writer's retreat we were invited to, and believe us, we attempted to talk ourselves out of going. Health concerns, work pressures, daily stressors and the demands of everyday life almost held us back from the life-changing path crossing God had planned for us. Despite rational excuses to opt out, we both said "yes" anyway. And boy are we glad.

Divine appointments matter and ours was one. We couldn't have imagined the domino effect that our first face-to-face meeting would create that would lead to the kingdom work we both now get the opportunity to do, together. We wouldn't be where we are without God, and the glory goes all to Him. Every step we take, every word we type, every woman we touch, every retreat we coordinate, every single thing we do is done for Him and for His purpose. God, thank you for loving us, for guiding us and for trusting us to this calling. We don't take it lightly.

When we decided to listen to the Holy Spirit's nudge to bring together our unique skills and talents to serve Christian women through this ministry, we were reminded of the surround-sound effect sweat equity has on all parts of our lives, families included. Our husbands and children, as well as extended family and friends, have cheered us on despite the late nights, early mornings, days away and Spirit-led impromptu life shifts. They have poured confidence in us when ours wavered. They have created margin so we could follow God's path for us. They have celebrated our successes with us, and best of all, they have glorified God alongside us, seeing His work in all of us. To David, Cory, Reid, Evan, Eli, Lyndi and

Luke, we love you all more than words could ever capture. Your support of our work—and our motherhood journeys—means everything to us.

We both have others who have shaped who we are including the mothers we desire to be and the women in Christ we are called to be. The matriarchs in our lives, the mothers who walk alongside us, the mothers before us we will never know and the mothers we are raising or look forward to meeting one day—our lives are changed because of you... because of the mothers you were or will be.

So many amazing people have supported us in bringing our ministry to life. To the women who have attended our retreats, invited us to come to speak to their communities, listened to our podcasts, read our books, supported our ministry through prayer and so much more, thank you! We see you, and we are so grateful for you. To those who helped bring this book to life—our cover designer, editor, graphic designer, web developer and more—thank you for helping us in our mission to bring more women to a deeper connection with God.

Finally, to the eight women who are highlighted in this book: Sarah, Hagar, Jochebed, Bathsheba, Mary, Elizabeth, the Shunammite woman and the Canaanite woman. Each of you may not have felt seen. You may have experienced loneliness, moments of feeling misunderstood or thoughts of shame or guilt. Worry likely followed you and yet, we see you. We are grateful for you. Thank you for listening to God's calling in your life and showing us that God takes broken women and helps use them for a beautiful purpose. We are better mothers because of you.

ABOUT THE AUTHORS

Meet Stephanie and Shannon.
Two women with one shared mission.

They are on the path of doing kingdom work and empowering Christian women to deepen their relationship with their Maker.

Both authors found themselves at a writers retreat, unaware that their time together would be a divine appointment. But just because they weren't aware of God's plan didn't mean God hadn't orchestrated their paths crossing. There, the two uncovered their mutual love for Jesus, their passion for writing and a budding friendship that was destined for more. They always knew God had a plan for their paths to merge, but both got goosebumps when they realized Broken & Beautiful Retreats, LLC may be His way.

Nearly a year after meeting, Shannon unexpectedly received a call from Stephanie, not a normal occurrence by any stretch of the imagination. That call poised an opportunity. "Hey Shannon, what do you think of hosting a women's retreat with me in a few weeks?" Stephanie felt the Holy Spirit nudge her to dial Shannon's number before canceling a reservation at a retreat facility she had planned to use for other business purposes. After some prayer, the ladies said yes to God's nudge, and the rest is history, a part of His story, actually.

What was meant to be one beautiful, Spirit-filled women's retreat turned into a purpose-filled ministry these two women couldn't have planned for, but one they are both eternally grateful for.

Shannon Carroll

Shannon grew up in a Christian family and the Church, but it took broken experiences of miscarriages, PTSD and her husband's stress-induced amnesia to bring her to a place of purpose. She serves as a pastor's wife and approaches life often through her lens as a registered nurse and wellness educator. Shannon knew from the first time she met Stephanie that God had something super special planned for their relationship. She is also the author of *One Thing Remains: One Couple's Traumatic Encounter with Amnesia and Their Life-Changing Journey to Restoration* and its companion, *One Thing Remains: 7-Week Guided Bible Study*.

Stephanie Feger

A woman of faith her whole life, it was middle-of-the-night moments that changed her life's trajectory. In the thick of pregnancy insomnia and work stress, Stephanie found her fingertips on the keyboard, capturing her conversations with God. Those writings were the beginning of a book, *Color Today Pretty: An Inspirational Guide to Living a Life in Perspective*; that book the beginning of a business; and that business the beginning of many relationships, including the one that invited her to meet Shannon. Stephanie is also the author of the companion, *Color Today Pretty Guided Journal*, and other books including *Emergence: Living Lessons from the Soil* and *Make Your Author emPact: Sell More Books, Increase Your Reach & Achieve Your Why*. She is also the founder of the emPower PR Group, a boutique book marketing solution for Christian nonfiction authors.

Women of Redemption: Motherhood Wisdom from 8 Biblical Matriarchs is Shannon and Stephanie's first book together and is the beginning of a series.

ABOUT BROKEN & BEAUTIFUL RETREATS, LLC

Embrace the broken.
Empower the beautiful.
Experience breakthroughs.

Far from perfect, we are all a broken people searching for mortar to fill in our gaps from the cracks that pain and hardships create. Many women feel discouraged, defeated, worried, filled with concern and overwhelm.

Brokenness can do that to anyone.
But it doesn't have to.

Something amazing can happen at the exact spot where brokenness lives. There lies the potential for something incredible; the gift to piece all parts of us back together in a way that makes us more beautiful and even stronger than before. Our Savior is our mortar. He helps us transform through our hardships to be a beautiful representation of His image and likeness. No brokenness is too messy for Him; no hardship too big.

Broken & Beautiful Retreats, LLC offers Christian women an intentional and Spirit-led pause to reconnect, recalibrate and rejuvenate. We were made for community; we learn from one another, and our brokenness is at the heart of what connects us. This is at the foundation of Broken & Beautiful Retreats, LLC, a ministry founded and co-led by Shannon Carroll and Stephanie Feger. Together, they host women's retreats, collaborate with groups to bring their unique experiences to their communities, host Bible studies and share their real-world biblical insights with women through keynotes, work-shops, podcasts and more.

Learn more about how you can experience a broken and beautiful breakthrough by inviting Shannon and Stephanie to create a custom experience for your community, attend an upcoming Broken & Beautiful Retreat or learn how you can support their ministry by visiting www.BrokenandBeautifulRetreats.com.

www.ingramcontent.com/pod-product-compliance
Lightning Source LLC
Chambersburg PA
CBHW070702130626
46553CB00005B/1808